Every Lady Her Own Flower Gardener

Addressed to the Industrious and Economical

Louisa Johnson

APPLEWOOD BOOKS
Bedford, Massachusetts

Every Lady Her Own Flower Gardener
was originally published in

1863

9781429013840

Thank you for purchasing an Applewood book.
Applewood reprints America's lively classics—
books from the past that are still of interest
to the modern reader.
For a free copy of a catalog of our
bestselling books, write to us at:
Applewood Books
Box 365
Bedford, MA 01730
or visit us on the web at:
awb.com

Prepared for publishing by HP

EVERY LADY

Her Own Flower Gardener.

ADDRESSED TO THE

INDUSTRIOUS AND ECONOMICAL.

CONTAINING

SIMPLE AND PRACTICAL DIRECTIONS

FOR

CULTIVATING PLANTS AND FLOWERS

IN THE GARDEN AND IN ROOMS.

BY LOUISA JOHNSON.

Revised from the Fourteenth London Edition, and Adapted to the

USE OF AMERICAN LADIES.

C. M. SAXTON, PUBLISHER,
25 PARK ROW, NEW YORK,
1863.

PUBLISHER'S ADVERTISEMENT

THE Publisher, having found the want of small, cheap Books of acknowledged merit, on the great topics of farming economy, and meeting for those of such a class a constant demand, offers, in his Rural Handbooks, of which this is one, works calculated to fill the void.

He trusts that a discerning Public will both buy and read these little Treatises, so admirably adapted to all classes, and fitted by their size for the pocket, and thus readable at the fireside, on the road, and in short everywhere.

C. M. SAXTON,

Agricultural Book Publisher.

I HAVE been induced to compile this little work from hearing many of my companions regret that no single book contained a sufficiently condensed and general account of the business of a Flower Garden. "We require," they said, "a work in a small compass, which will enable us to become our own gardener; we wish to know how to set about everything *ourselves*, without expense, without being deluged with Latin words and technical terms, and without being obliged to pick our way through multiplied publications, redolent of descriptions, and not always particularly lucid. We require a practical work, telling us of useful flowers, simple modes of rearing them, simply expressed, and free from lists of plants and roots which require expensive methods of preservation. Some of us have gardens, but we cannot afford a gardener; we like flowers, but we cannot attempt to take more than common pains to raise them. We require to know the hardiest flowers, and to comprehend the general business of the garden, undisturbed by fear of failure, and at the most economical scale of expense. Who will write us such a book?"

I have endeavored to meet their views; and my plan of Floriculture may be carried into effect by any lady who can command the services of an old man, a woman, or a stout boy. In the present Edition, the publishers have added a paper on WINDOW GARDENING, written by Mr. M'Intosh—and another on DOMESTIC GREENHOUSES, an apparatus by which a small collection of exotics may be given in great perfection, and by a process which any lady may superintend with much gratification. In every other respect the work is the result of my own experience, and I dedicate it to all of my own sex who delight in flowers, and yet cannot allow themselves to enter into great expense in their cultivation.

LOUISA JOHNSON.

CONTENTS.

CHAPTER I.

INTRODUCTION.

CHAPTER II.

GENERAL REMARKS.

CHAPTER III.

LAYING OUT.

CHAPTER IV.

BULBS AND PERENNIALS.

CHAPTER V

ANNUALS.

CHAPTER VI.

ROSES AND JASMINES.

CHAPTER VII.

SHRUBS AND EVERGREENS.

CHAPTER VIII.

ON HOUSE AND WINDOW GARDENING.

CHAPTER IX.

DOMESTIC GREENHOUSES.

CHAPTER X.

MONTHLY NOTICES.

LADIES FLOWER GARDENER.

CHAPTER I.

INTRODUCTION.

IT has been well remarked that a garden affords the purest of human pleasures. The study of Nature is interesting in all her manifold combinations: in her wildest attitudes, and in her artful graces. The mind is amused, charmed, and astonished in turn, with contemplating her inexhaustible display; and we worship the God who created such pure and simple blessings for his creatures. These blessings are open to all degrees and conditions of men. Nature is not a boon bestowed upon the high-born, or purchased by the wealthy at a kingly price. The poor, the blind, the halt, and the diseased, enjoy her beauty, and derive benefit from her study. Every cottager enjoys the little garden which furnishes his table with comforts, and his mind with grateful feelings, if that mind is susceptible of religious impressions. He contemplates the gracious Providence which has bestowed such means of enjoyment upon him, as the Father whose all-seeing eye provides for the lowliest of his children; and who has placed the "purest of human pleasures" within the reach of all who are not too blind to behold his mercy. With this blessed view before his mental sight, the cottager cultivates his little homestead. The flowers and fruits of the earth bud, bloom, and decay in their season; but Nature again performs her deputed mission, and spring succeeds the dreary winter with renewed beauty and two-fold increase. Health accompanies simple and natural pleasures. The culture of the ground affords a vast and interminable field of observation, in which the mind ranges with singular pleasure, though the body travels not. It surrounds home with an unceasing interest; domestic scenes become endeared to the eye and mind; worldly cares recede; and we may truly say—

"For us kind Nature wakes her genial power,
Suckles each herb, and spreads out every flower!
Annual for us, the grape, the rose, renew
The juice nectarious, and the balmy dew:
For us, the mine a thousand treasures brings;
For us, health gushes from a thousand springs."
Eth. ep. i. ver. 129.

The taste for gardening in England began to display itself in the reign of Edward III., in whose time the first work on the subject was composed by Walter de Henly. Flower-gardening followed slowly in its train. The learned Linacre, who died in 1524, introduced the damask rose from Italy into England. King James I. of Scotland, when a prisoner in Windsor Castle, thus describes its "most faire" garden:—

"Now was there maide fast by the towris wall,
A garden faire, and in the corneris set
An herbere green, with wandis long and small
Railit about,-and so with treeis set
Was all the place, and hawthorn hedges knet,
That lyfe was now, walking, there forbye,
That might within scarce any wight espie,
So thick the bowis and the leves grene
Bercandit all, the alleyes all that there were;
And myddis every herbere might be sene
The scharpe grene swete junipere
Growing so fair, with branches here and there,
That, as it seymt to a lyfe without,
The bowis spred the herbere all about."
The Quair.

Henry VIII. ordered the formation of his garden at Nonsuch about the year 1509, and Leland says it was a "Nonpareil."

Hentyner assures us of its perfect beauty, describing one of its marble basins as being set round with "lilac trees, which trees bear no fruit, but only a pleasant smell."

The pleasure-gardens at Theobalds, the seat of Lord Burleigh, were unique, according to the report of Lyson. In it were nine knots exquisitely made, one of which was set forth in likeness of the king's arms. "One might walk two myle in the walks before he came to an end."

Queen Elizabeth was extremely fond of flowers, and her taste ever influenced that of her court. Gilliflowers, carnations, tulips, Provence and musk roses, were brought to England in her reign.

William III. loved a pleasaunce or pleasure-garden; but he introduced the Dutch fashion of laying them out, which is still horrible in our eyes. His Queen superintended in person all her arrangements in the flower-garden,—an amusement particularly delightful to her. In those days, "knottes and mazes" were no longer the pride of a parterre, with a due allowance of "pleasant and fair fishponds."

Queen Anne remodeled the gardens at Kensington, and did away with the Dutch inventions. Hampton Court was also laid out in a more perfect state in her reign, under the direction of Wise.

Since that period, flower-gardening has progressed rapidly; and the amusement of floriculture has become the dominant passion of the ladies of Great Britain. It is a passion most blessed in its effects, considered as an amusement or a benefit: Nothing humanizes and adorns the female mind more surely than a taste for ornamental gardening. It compels the reason to act, and the judgment to observe; it is favorable to meditation of the most serious kind; it exercises the fancy in harmless and elegant occupation, and braces the system by its healthful tendency. A flower-garden, to the young and single of my sex, acts upon the heart and affections as a nursery acts upon the matronly feelings. It attaches them to their home; it throws a powerful charm over the spot dedicated to such deeply-interesting employment; and it lures them from dwelling too deeply upon the unavoidable disappointments and trials of life, which sooner or later disturb and disquiet the heart.

An amusement which kings and princes have stamped with dignity, and which has afforded them recreation under the toils of government, must become for ever venerated, and will be sought for by every elegant as well as by every scientific mind. Floriculture ranges itself under the head of female accomplishments in these our days; and we turn with pity from the spirit which will not find in her "garden of roses" the simplest and purest of pleasures.

CHAPTER II.

GENERAL REMARKS.

IN the laying out of a garden, the soil and situation must be considered as much as the nature of the ground will admit. Let no lady, however, despair of being able to raise fine flowers upon any soil, providing the sun is not too much excluded, for the rays of the sun are the vital principle of existence to all vegetation. The too powerful rays can be warded off by the arts of invention, but we have yet no substitute for that glorious orb. Unless its warm and forcing influence is allowed to extend over the surface of the garden, all flowers wither, languish, and die. Sun and air are the lungs and heart of flowers. A lady will be rewarded for her trouble in making her parterre in the country; but in large towns, under the influence of coal smoke, shade, and gloom, her lot will be constant disappointment. She can only hope to keep a few consumptive geraniums languishing through the summer months, to die in October, and show the desolating view of rows of pots containing blackened and dusty stems.

Many soils which are harsh or arid, are susceptible of improvement by a little pains. Thus, a stiff clay, by digging well and leaving it to become pulverized by the action of the frost, and then mixing plenty of ashes with it, becomes a fine mould, which I have ever found most excellent for all flowers of the hardier kind. The black soil is the richest in itself, and requires no assistance beyond changing it about a foot in depth every three years, as a flower garden requires renewing, if a lady expects a succession of handsome flowers. The ground should be well dug the latter end of September or October, or even in November, and if the soil is not sufficiently fine, let it be dug over a second or third time, and neatly raked with a very fine-toothed rake.

Stony ground requires riddling well, and great care must be taken to keep it neat by picking up the little stones which constantly force themselves to the surface after rains. Nothing is so unbecoming as weeds and stones in parterres, where the eye seeks flowers and neatness.

Almost every plant loves sand; and if that can be procured, it enriches and nourishes the soil, especially for bulbs, pinks, carnations, auriculas, hyacinths, &c. Let it be mixed in the proportion of a third part to the whole.

If the dead leaves are swept into a mound every autumn, and the soap suds, brine, &c., of the house be thrown upon it, the mass will quickly decompose, and become available the following year. It makes an admirable compost for auriculas, &c., mixed with garden or other mould.

If the ground be a gravelly soil, the flower-garden should not slope, for stony ground requires all the moisture you can give it, while the sloping situation would increase the heat and dryness. A moist earth, on the contrary, would be improved by being sloped towards the east or west.

The south is not so proper for flowers, as a glaring sun withers the tender flowers; but the north must be carefully avoided, and shut out by a laurel hedge, a wall, or any rural fence garnished with hardy creepers, or monthly roses, which make a gay and agreeable defense. Monthly roses are invaluable as auxiliaries of all kinds. They will grow in any soil, and bloom through the winter months, always giving a delicate fragrance, and smiling even in the snow. Monthly roses will ever be the florist's delight: they are the hardiest, most delicate-looking, and greenest leaved of garden productions; they give no trouble, and speedily form a beautiful screen against any offensive object. No flower garden should exist without abundance of monthly roses.

It has often been a disputed point whether flower gardens should be intersected with gravel walks or with grass plots. This must be left entirely to the taste and means of the party forming a garden. Lawn is as wet and melancholy in the winter months, as it is beautiful and desirable in summer; and it requires great care and attention in mowing and rolling, and trimming round the border. Gravel walks have this advantage: the first trouble is the last. They will only require an old woman's or a child's assistance in keeping them free from weeds; and a lady has not the same fears of taking cold, or getting wet in her feet, during the rains of autumn and spring.

Many females are unequal to the fatigue of bending down to flowers, and particularly object to the stooping posture. In this case, ingenuity alone is required to raise the flowers to a convenient height; and, by so doing, to increase the beauty and picturesque appearance of the garden. Old barrels cut in half, tubs, pails, &c., neatly painted outside, or adorned with rural ornaments, and raised upon feet neatly carved, or mounds of earth, stand in lieu of richer materials, such as vases, parapet walls, and other expensive devices, which ornament the gardens of the wealthy. I have seen these humble materials shaped into forms as pleasing to the eye, and even more consonant to our damp climate, than marble vases. They never look green from time, and are renewed at a very trifling expense. A few pounds of nails, and the unbarked thinnings from fir plantations, are the sole requisites towards forming any device which a tasteful fancy can dictate; and a little green paint adds beauty and durability when the bark falls from the wood it protects. I have seen fir balls nailed on to these forms in tasteful patterns; and creepers being allowed to fall gracefully over the brims, give a remarkably pleasing and varied appearance to the parterre.

Where mould is not easily to be procured—as, for instance, in towns—the tubs or receptacles may be half filled with any kind of rubble, only space must be left to allow of two feet of fine mould at the top, which is quite sufficient for bulbous roots, creepers, &c. These receptacles have one powerful advantage over ground plots; they can be moved under sheds, or into outhouses, during the heavy rains or frosts of winter; and thereby enable a lady to preserve the more delicate flowers, which would deteriorate by constant exposure to inclement weather.

A lady requires peculiar tools for her light work. She should possess a light spade; two rakes, one with very fine teeth, and the other a size larger, for cleaning the walks when they are raked, and for raking the larger stones from the garden borders. A light garden fork is very necessary to take up bulbous or other roots with, as the spade would wound and injure them, whereas they pass safely through the interstices of the fork or prong. A watering-pot is indispensable, and a hoe. Two trowels are likewise necessary; one should be a tolerable size, to transplant perennial and biennial flower roots; the other should be pointed and small, to transplant the more delicate roots of anemones, bulbs, &c.

The pruning-knife must be always sharp, and, in shape, it should bend a little inwards, to facilitate cutting away straggling or dead shoots, branches, &c. The "avroncator," lately so much in request, is an admirable instrument; but it is expensive, and of most importance in shrubberies, where heavy branches are to be cut away. The Sieur Louis d'Auxerre, who wrote a work upon gardening in 1706, has a sketch of the avroncator of the present day, which he designates as caterpillar shears.

A light pair of shears, kept always in good order, is necessary to keep privet or laurel hedges properly clipped; and a stout deep basket must be deposited in the tool-shed, to contain the weeds and clippings. These are the only tools absolutely *essential* to a lady's garden. I have seen a great variety decorating the wall of an amateur tool-house, but they must have been intended for show, not for use. A real artiste, in whatever profession she may engage, will only encumber herself with essentials. All else is superfluous.

I have reserved two especially necessary recommendations to the last, being comforts independent of the tool-house. Every lady should be furnished with a gardening apron, composed of stout Holland, with ample pockets to contain her pruning-knife, a small stout hammer, a ball of string, and a few nails and snippings of cloth. Have nothing to do with scissors; they are excellent in the work-room, but dangerous in a flower garden, as they wrench and wound the stems of flowers. The knife cuts slanting, which is the proper way of taking off slips; and the knife is sufficient for all the purposes of a flower garden, even for cutting string.

The second article which I pronounce to be indispensable is a pair of India rubber shoes, or the wooden high-heeled shoes called "sabots" by the French. In these protections, a lady may indulge her passion for flowers at all seasons, without risk of rheumatism or chills, providing it does not actually rain or snow: and the cheering influence of the fresh air, combined with a favorite amusement, must ever operate beneficially on the mind and body in every season of the year.

CHAPTER III.

ON LAYING OUT.

THERE are many modes of adorning a small piece of ground, so as to contain gay flowers and plants, and appear double its real size. By covering every wall or palisade with monthly roses and creepers of every kind, no space is lost, and unsightly objects even contribute to the general effect of a "Plaisaunce." The larger flowers, such as hollyhocks, sunflowers, &c., look to the best advantage as a back ground, either planted in clumps, or arranged singly. Scarlet lychnis, campanula, or any second-sized flowers, may range themselves below, and so in graduated order, till the eye reposes upon a foreground of pansies, auriculas, polyanthuses, and innumerable humbler beauties. Thus all are seen in their order, and present a mass of superb coloring to the observer, none interfering with the other. The hollyhock does not shroud the lowly pansy from displaying its bright tints of yellow and purple ; neither can the sturdy and gaudy sunflower hide the modest double violet or smartly clad anemone from observation. Each flower is by this mode of planting distinctly seen, and each contributes its beauty and its scent, by receiving the beams of the sun in equal proportions.

If the trunk of a tree stands tolerably free from deep overshadowing branches, twine the creeping rose, the late honeysuckle, or the everlasting pea round its stem, that every inch of ground may become available. The tall naked stem of the young ash looks well festooned with roses and honeysuckles.

Wherever creeping flowering plants can live, let them adorn every nook and corner, stem, wall, and post; they are elegant in appearance, and many of them, particularly clematis, are delicious in fragrant scent.

If flowers are planted in round or square plots, the same rule applies in arranging them. The tallest must be placed in the center, but I recommend a lady to banish sunflowers and hollyhocks from her plots, and consign them to broad borders against a wall, or in clumps of three and three, as a screen against the north, or against any unsightly object. Their large roots draw so much nourishment from the ground, that the lesser plants suffer, and the soil becomes quickly exhausted. Like gluttons, they should feed alone, or their companions will languish in starvation, and become impoverished. The wren cannot feed with the vulture.

The south end or corner of a moderate flower garden should be fixed upon for the erection of a root house, which is not an expensive undertaking, and which forms a picturesque as well as a most useful appendage to a lady's parterre. Thinnings of plantations, which are everywhere procured at a very moderate charge, rudely shaped and nailed into any fancied form, may supply all that is needful to the little inclosure; and a thatch of straw, rushes, or heather, will prove a sure defense to the roof and back. There, a lady may display her taste by the beauty of the flowers which she may train through the rural frame-work. There, the moss-rose, the jessamine, the honeysuckle, the convolvulus, and many other bright and beautiful flowers, may escape and cluster around her, as she receives rest and shelter within their graceful lattice-work. There, also, may be deposited the implements of her vocation; and during the severe weather, its warm precincts will protect the finer kinds of carnations, pinks, auriculas, &c., which do not bear the heavy rains, or frosts of lengthened duration, without injuring the plant.

Flowers are divided into three classes:—annuals, biennials, and perennials.

Annuals are those flowers which are raised from seeds alone, in the spring, and which die in the autumn. They are again divided into three classes:—the tender and more curious kinds; the less tender or hardier kinds; and the hardiest and common kinds.

Biennials are those flowers which are produced by seed, bloom the second year, and remain two years in perfection, after which they gradually dwindle and die away.

Some sorts, however, of the biennials, afford a continuation of plants by offsets, slips, and cuttings of the tops, and by layers and pipings, so that, though the parent flower dies, the species are perpetuated, particularly to continue curious double-flowered kinds, as for instance, double rockets, by root offsets, and cuttings of the young flower-stalks; double wallflowers by slips of the small top shoots; double sweet-williams by layers and pipings; and carnations by layers.

Perennials are those flowers which continue many years, and are propagated by root offsets, suckers, parting roots, &c., as will be more fully particularised under the head of *Perennials*.

It has been a debated point among florists whether plots or baskets should be devoted each to a particular variety of flower, or receive flowers of different kinds, flowering at separate seasons. Thus, many ladies set apart one plot of ground for anemones only —another plot receives only pansies, and so on. There is much to be said on both sides the question.

If a plot of ground is devoted to one variety of flower only, you can give it the appropriate mould, and amuse your eye with its expanse of bright coloring. Nothing is more beautiful than a bed of pansies, or a bed of the bright and glowing scarlet verbina; nothing can exceed the gay and flaunty tints of a bed of tulips, or the rich hues of the lilac and the white petunia. A large space of garden allows its possessor to revel in separate beds of flowers, whose beauty is increased twofold by masses; and from that very space, the eye does not so easily discover the melancholy appearance of one or more plots exhibiting nothing but dark mould, and withered stems, arising from the earlier sorts being out of bloom.

But in less spacious gardens, this gloomy and mournful vacuum must be avoided. Every border and plot of ground should exhibit a gay succession of flowers in bloom; and that object can only be effected by a pretty equal distribution of flowers of early and late growth. As the May flowers droop, the June productions supply their place; and these, again, are followed in succession, till the Golden rod and Michaelmas day daisy announce the decadence of the parterre for the year.

Yet every flower may be supplied with its favorite soil with a little patience and observation. A light soil suits all descriptions very well; and I never yet found disappointment in any description of earth which was thoroughly well dug, and dressed yearly from the mound of accumulated leaves and soap-suds, alluded to in the first chapter. I particularly recommend a portion of sand mixed with the heap. All bulbs, carnations, pinks, auriculas, ranunculuses, &c., love a mixture of sand. I know no flowers of the hardy class which reject it. Mix sand well into your borders and plots, and you will not fail to have handsome flowers.

I subjoin a list of common flowers appertaining to each month, in order to fill the borders with one or more roots of each variety. I do not include the annuals.

JANUARY.

In this month the following flowers are in blow:—

Single Anemones	Primroses
Winter Cyclamens	Winter Hyacinth
Michaelmas Daisy	Narcissus of the East
Hepaticas	Christmas Rose

FEBRUARY.

Single Anemones	Single Yellow Gilliflower
Forward Anemones	Single Liverwort
Persian Iris	Winter Aconite
Spring Crocus	Hepaticas

MARCH.

Bulbous Iris	Hyacinths of all sorts
Anemones of all sorts	Jonquils
Spring Cyclamens	Yellow Gilliflower
Liverwort of all sorts	Narcissus of several kinds
Daffodils	Forward Bears'-ears
Crowfoots	Forward Tulips
Spring Crocus	Single Primroses of divers colors

APRIL.

Daisies	Double Liverworts
Yellow Gilliflowers	Primroses
Narcissus of all sorts	Honeysuckles
Forward Bears'-ear	Tulips
Spring Cyclamens	Hyacinths
Crocus, otherwise called Saffron-flowers	Single Jonquils
	Crown-Imperial
Anemones of all sorts	Yellow Gilliflowers, double and single
Iris	Pasque-Flowers
Pansies	March Violets
Daffodils	

MAY.

Anemones	Mountain Pinks
Gilliflowers of all sorts	Pansies
Yellow Gilliflowers	Peonies of all sorts
Columbines	Ranunculuses of all sorts
Asphodils	Some Irises: as those which we call the Bulbous Iris, and the Chamæ-Iris
Orange, or flame-colored Lilies	
Double Jacea, a sort of Lychnis	
Cyanuses of all sorts	Italian Spiderwort, a sort of Asphodil
Hyacinths	
Day Lilies	Poet's Pinks
Bastard Dittany	Backward Tulips
Daisies	Julians, otherwise called English Gilliflowers
Lily of the Valley	

JUNE.

Snap-dragons of all sorts
Wild Tansies
Pinks, otherwise called Lychnises
Irises
Roses
Tuberoses
Pansies
Larkspur
Great Daisies
Climbers
Cyanuses of all sorts
Foxgloves of all sorts
Mountain Lilies
Gilliflowers of all sorts
Monk's-hoods
Pinks of all sorts
Candy-tufts
Poppies

JULY.

Jessamine
Spanish Brown
Basils
Bell-flowers
Indian Jacea
Great Daisies
Monk's-hoods
Pinks
Scabiuses
Nigellas
Cyclamens
Lobel's Catch-flies
Lilies of all sorts
Apples of Love
Comfrey
Poppies
Snap-dragons
Double Marigolds
Amaranthuses
Hellebore
Ox-eyes
Pinks of the Poets
Bee-flowers
Sea-hollies
Foxgloves
Wild Poppies
Everlastings
Roses
Dittanies
Bindweeds
Lilies of St. Bruno
Tricolors
Squills
Motherworts
Climbers
Oculus Christi
Camomile
Sunflowers
Belvederes
Gilliflowers of all sorts
Thorn-apple
Valerian

AUGUST.

Oculus Christi, otherwise called Starwort
Belvederes
Climbers of all sorts
Apples of Love
Marvels of Peru
Pansies
Ranunculuses
Double Marigolds
Candy-tufts
Autumn Cyclamens
Jessamines
Sunflowers, vivacious and annual
Indian Narcissus
Foxgloves
Cyclamens
Passion-flowers
Everlastings
Tuberoses
Monk's-hood
Indian Pinks of all kinds
Bindweed
Passvelours
Great Daisies
White Bell-flower
Autumnal Meadow Saffron
Gilliflowers

SEPTEMBER.

Tricolors	Amaryllis
Love-apples	Autumnal Narcissus
Marvel of Peru	White Bell-flowers
Monk's-hood	Indian Pinks
Narcissus of Portugal	Indian Roses
Snap-dragons	Amaranthus
Oculus Christi	Pansies
Basils	Passion-flower
Belvederes	Autumnal Crocus
Great Daisies	Thorn-apple
Double Marigolds	Carnations
Monthly Roses	Ranunculuses planted in May
Tuberoses	Colchicums

OCTOBER.

Tricolors	Pansies that were sown in August
Oculus Christi	Passion-flower
Snap-dragons	Passvelours
Colchicums	Double Marigolds
Autumn Crocus	Some Pinks
Autumnal Cyclamens	Amaryllis
Monk's-hood	Autumnal Narcissus
Indian Pinks	

NOVEMBER.

Snap-dragons	Double Violets
Double and Single Gilliflowers	Single Anemones of all sorts
Great Daisies	Winter Cyclamens
Pansies sown in August	Forward Hellebore
Monthly Roses	Golden Rod

Rabbits are an intolerable nuisance in a flower garden, and in some country places they abound most destructively. A light wire fence about two feet high, closely lattice-worked, or a net of the same height, carried round the garden, is a sure defense from these marauders. But where these conveniences are unattainable, there are other modes which answer the purpose, but they require a little trouble and patience.

It is the well-known nature of Rabbits and Hares to dislike climbing or entangling their feet; and very simple inventions deter them from attempting to gnaw the roots and hearts of flowers. They will not walk upon straw or ashes strewed thickly round any plant: they equally dislike a fence of sticks placed round a plot, with bits of white paper or card fastened to each stick; or a string carried round the sticks a foot or two high. If they cannot creep under a slight fence, they never attempt to leap over it. If a stick is run into the ground close to a plant, and other sticks are slanted from the ground towards the center, the plant will remain untouched, be the frost of ever so long duration.

Snails are disagreeable intruders, but the following method is an exterminating war of short duration:—

Throw cabbage leaves upon your borders over night; in the morning, early, you will find them covered underneath with snails, which have taken refuge there. Thus they are easily taken and destroyed.

Earwigs are taken in great numbers by hanging gallipots, tubes, or any such receptacle, upon low sticks in the borders over night. In these they shelter themselves, and are consequently victimized in the morning. The gallipots, broken bottles, &c., should be placed upon the stick like a man's hat, that the vermin may ascend into them.

Ants are very great enemies to flowers; but I know no method of attacking them, except in their own strongholds, which I have always done with cruel intrepidity and success. My only plan was to lay open the little ant-hill, and pour boiling water upon the busy insects, which destroyed at once the commonwealth, and the eggs deposited within the mound. In some places ants are extremely large and abundant, and they quickly destroy the beauty of a flower by attacking its root and heart.*

* The Emperor Pagonatus, who wrote a treatise upon agriculture, assures us, that to clear a garden of ants, we should burn empty snail shells with storax wood, and throw the ashes upon the ant-hills, which obliges them to remove. I never tried this method.

Mildew and blight infest roses and honey-suckles. Soap-suds thrown over rose bushes; heavy waterings with tobacco-water, or the water in which potatoes have been boiled, is successful in a degree, but the best way is a very troublesome one to persevere in. Pinch every leaf well which curls up, by which you may know a small maggot is deposited therein. By so doing you destroy the germ of a thousand little monsters.

Mildew and blight come from the east; therefore honeysuckles should be sheltered from that aspect; for, as they rise and spread widely, they are not so manageable as a rose-bush. A mass of luxuriant honeysuckles is beautiful to the eye and delicious in fragrance: but covered with mildew, it is a blackened and miserable object. Mildew, fortunately, does not make its appearance every spring; but once in four or five years it comes as a plague, to desolate the garden. A great deal may be raked away if taken off as soon as it spreads its cobwebs over these lovely flowers; but it should be done without delay.

I cannot lay too great stress upon the neatness in which a lady's garden should be kept. If it is not beautifully neat, it is nothing. For this reason, keep every plant distinct in the flower-beds; let every tall flower be well staked, that the wind may not blow it prostrate; rake away dead leaves from the beds, and trim every flower-root from discolored leaves, weeds, &c.; remove all weeds and stones the moment they appear, and clear away decaying stems, which are so littering and offensive to the eye. There is always some employment of this kind for every week in the year.

Old iron rods, both large and small, are to be procured cheap at the ironmongers. These old rusty rods, painted green, or lead color, are excellent stakes for supporting flowers, and do not wear out. The slighter rods are very firm upright supporters for Carnations, Pinks, &c., while the taller and larger rods are the firmest and best poles for hollyhocks, sunflowers, and the larger class of plants. Fix the flower stem to its stake with string, or the tape of the bass matting, soaked in water to prevent its cracking, and tie it sufficiently tight to prevent the wind tearing it from its position. Tie the large stems in three places for security.

The term *Deciduous*, applied to shrubs, signifies that they shed their leaves every winter.

Herbaceous plants, signify those plants whose roots are not woody, such as stocks, wallflowers, &c. &c.

Fibrous-rooted plants, are those whose roots shoot out small fibers, such as Polyanthuses, violets, &c.

Tuberous-rooted plants, signify those roots which form and grow into little tubes, such as Anemones, Ranunculuses, &c.

PERENNIALS.

Perennials are flowers of many years' duration; and they multiply themselves most abundantly by suckers, offsets, parting the roots, &c. They require little trouble beyond taking care to renew the soil every year or two by a somewhat plentiful supply from the compost heap; and by separating the offsets, and parting the roots in autumn, to strengthen the mother plant. When the flowers are past and the stems have decayed, then the operation may take place. Choose a showery day for transplanting the roots, or give them a moderate watering to fix them in their fresh places. When you transplant a flower root, dig a hole with your trowel sufficiently large to give the fibers room to lie freely and evenly in the ground.

I have, throughout my little work, laid great stress upon possessing a heap of compost, ready to apply to roots and shrubs every spring and autumn. Wherever the soil is good the flowers will bloom handsomely; and no lady will be disappointed of that pleasure, if a compost heap forms one essential, in a hidden corner of the flower garden. If you raise your perennials from seed, sow it in the last week in March in a bed of light earth, in the open ground. Let the bed be in a genial, warm situation, and divide it into small compartments; a compartment for each sort of seed.

Sow the seed thin, and rake or break the earth over them finely. Let the larger seed be sown half an inch deep, and the smaller seed a quarter of an inch. Water the beds in dry weather often with a watering pot, not a jug. The rose of the watering pot distributes the water equally among the seedlings; whereas, water dashed upon them from a jug falls in masses, and forms holes in the light earth, besides prostrating the delicate seedling.

About the end of May, the seedlings will be fit to remove into another nursery bed, to gain strength till October; or be planted at once where they are to remain. Put the plants six inches apart, and water them moderately, to settle the earth about their roots.

But it is rarely required to sow seed for perennial plants,—they multiply so vigorously and quickly of themselves, by offsets; and cuttings may be made of the flower stalks in May and June in profusion.

The double *Scarlet lychnis*, and those plants which rise with firm flower stems, make excellent cuttings, and grow freely when planted in moist weather. Double *Rockets*, *Lychnidea*, and many others, succeed well.

Carnation and *pink* seedlings must be taken great care of. They will be ready to plant out about the middle of June, and as innumerable varieties spring from sowing seed, they should be planted carefully in a bed by themselves six inches asunder, and they will flower the following year, when you can choose the colors you most approve. Carnations properly rank under the head of biennials; but pinks are strictly perennial plants, and much has been written upon this hardy and beautiful flower. It comes originally from a temperate climate, therefore the pink loves shade: the fervid sunbeams cause its flowers to languish and droop. You may give them an eastern aspect.

Be careful to watch pinks when they are budding, and do not allow two buds to grow side by side. Pinch off the smaller bud, which would only weaken its companion. Keep the plants free from decayed leaves, and gently stir the earth round them occasionally with your small trowel. This operation refreshes them. Stake them neatly, that they may not fall prostrate after rain.

If you wish to preserve any particular pink, let it grow in a pot, or upon a raised platform, that it may be placed beyond the reach of hares, rabbits, or poultry, and be more easily sheltered from long and severe frost or rains in winter, and from the dry heats in summer, either of which destroys the beauty of the flower. The pots can be sunk in the ground in fine weather. Do not hide your pinks among larger flowers: let them be distinctly seen. If you water pinks too much, their roots become rotten; and if you suffer them to be too dry, they become diseased. Beware of extremes. The best rule is to keep them just moist. A fine pink should not have sharp-pointed flower leaves; they should be round and even at their edges, and the colors should be well defined, not running one into the other. The flower should be large; it should possess a great many leaves, and form a sort of dome. Piping and slipping, is the most expeditious mode of propagating plants from any selected pink.

Pansies, violets, &c., are very easily propagated by parting the roots when the flowers are past. Pansies are very beautiful flowers; and cuttings of their young shoots will grow very freely if kept moist and shaded for some little time. By refreshing the soil every year, you insure large flowers. Pansies and violets bloom early in the spring.

Hepaticas must be parted like violets. They appear so very early in the year that no garden should exist without these gay and modest flowers. The leaves appear after the flower has past away.

The *Polyanthus* blooms among the early tribe. In planting this flower, be careful to insert the roots deep in the soil, so that the leaves may rest upon it, for the roots are produced high upon the stem, and those roots must be enabled to shoot into the soil. The polyanthus, like almost every other flower, loves a good soil, with a mixture of sand.

In dividing these fibrous-rooted perennial plants, take only the strong offsets, with plenty of fibers attached to them.

Polyanthuses, auriculas, double daisies, double camomile, London pride, violets, hepaticas, thrift, primroses, gentianella, &c., succeed well, taken up and divided in September, for they will all have done flowering by that time. Indeed, all perennial fibrous-rooted plants may be taken up in October to have their roots parted, and the soil refreshed round them.

Peonies, and all knob-rooted plants, should be taken up in October to part their roots and transplant them to their intended positions.

The saxifrage has very small roots, which are apt to be lost in borders if not very carefully looked after. Like the anemone, &c., sift the earth well for them.

Dahlias require a word or two upon their culture. They love sand, therefore allow them plenty of it, but do not put manure to their roots, which throws them into luxuriant leaf and stem, to the deterioration of the flower. Peat mould is good, if you can obtain it, to mix with the sand, as it assists the flower in developing stripes and spots. Train each plant upright, upon one stem only, and give it a strong stake to support its weight, which soon succumbs under gusts of wind. Plant them in open and airy places When the stems become black, take them up, separate the roots, and plunge them into a box of ashes, barley chaff, or sand, to protect them through the winter. Plant them out in May.

Dahlias grow from cuttings, which require care and a hot-bed to do well, but they multiply themselves very sufficiently without that trouble.

It is a great perfection to see every tall plant in a flower-garden well staked, and trimmed from dead straggling shoots. Let no branches trail upon the border, but, as in the ease of Chrysanthemums, cut away the lowest branches or shoots, that each plant may stand erect and neat in its order, without intermeddling in its neighbor's concerns. There will be plenty of employment all through the summer in watching the growth of your plants, in cutting away decayed stems, and trimming off dead leaves. Let nothing remain in the flower's way after the brightness of its bloom has past by : cut off the drooping flower before it runs to seed, which only tends to weaken the other flowers, and leave only the finest flower to produce seed on each plant.

Perennials grow remarkably fine always in newly turned-up ground, but they gradually degenerate if they are allowed to remain above two years without replacing the substance they have exhausted in the soil. Add every year to that substance, by liberal supplies from the compost heap.

Be careful to multiply your supply of jasmines, honeysuckles, &c., by cuttings in their due season.

I subjoin a list of the hardier sorts of fibrous rooted Perennials, eligible to adorn a garden, from which my readers may stock their borders.

LIST OF HARDY PERENNIALS.

Aster, or Starwort
Large blue Alpine
Common Starwort, or Michaelmas Daisy
Early Pyrenean
Blue Italian Starwort
Catesby's Starwort
Dwarf narrow-leaved Starwort
Midsummer Starwort
Autumnal white Starwort, with broad leaves
Tripolian Starwort
Divaricated-branched
Virginian Starwort, with spiked blue flowers
Early blue Starwort
Rose Starwort
Latest Starwort, large blue flowers
New England Starwort
Red-flowering
Apocynum, Dogsbane
Red-flowering
Orange-colored
Syrian
Arum, Italian large-veined leaf
Asclepias, Swallow-wort
White
Yellow
Astragalus, Milk-vetch
Alysson, White
Yellow
Violet
Borage, the Eastern
Bachelor's Button
Double red
Double white
Double Ragged Robin
Campanula, or Bell-flower
Double blue
Double white
Double blue, and white nettle-leaved
Caltha, double-flowered
Marigold
Cassia of Maryland
Pinks, double pheasant's eye
Dobson
Deptford
Cob white
Red cob
White stock
Damask
Mountain
Matted
Old man's head
Painted lady
Clove pink, and many other varieties
Stock July-flower, the Brompton
Double scarlet Brompton
Single scarlet
Purple
White Brompton
Queen stock
Purple double
Striped double
Single of each sort
Twickenham stock
Lichnidea, early blue
Spotted-stalked, with purple spikes of flowers
Virginia, with large umbels
Low trailing purple
Carolina, with stiff shining leaves, and deeper purple flowers
Cyanus, broad-leaved
Narrow-leaved
Lychnis, or Campion
Single scarlet lychnis
Double scarlet lychnis
Catchfly, double flowers
Hepaticas, single white
Single blue
Single red
Double red
Double blue
Lineria, toad flax
Purple
Yellow
Bee Larkspur
Fraxinella, white
Red
Gentiania, great yellow
Gentianella, blue
Globularia, blue daisy
Fox-glove, red
White
Iron-colored

Perennial Sun-flower
Double yellow, and several other species.
Cyclamen, red
White
Goldy Locks
Chelone, white
Red
Lily of the Valley, common
Double-flowering
Solomon's Seal, single
Double
Filapendula, or Dropwort
Columbines, common blue
Double red
Double white
Double striped
Starry, double and single
Early-flowering Canada
Thalictrum, feathered columbines
Pulsatilla, blue Pasque flower
Orobus, bitter vetch
Saxifrage, double white
Thick-leaved
Purple
Veronica, upright blue
Dwarf blue
Hungarian
Blush
Golden Rod, many species
Valerian, red garden Valerian
White garden
Rudbekia, American sun-flower
Dwarf Virginia, with large yellow flowers
Dwarf Carolina, with narrow red reflexed petals and purple florets
Virginia, with yellow rays and red florets
Tall yellow, with purple stalks and heart-shaped leaves
Taller, with yellow flowers and large five-lobed leaves, and those on the stalks single
Tallest yellow, with narrower leaves, which are all of five lobes
Pulmonaria, Lungwort
Common
American

Monarda, purple
Scarlet
Ephemeron, Spider-wort, or flowers of a day
White
Blue
Jucca, American knapweed
Primrose, double yellow
Double scarlet
White
Polyanthus, many varieties
Auriculas, many varieties
Violets, double blue
Double white
Double red
Russian
Banksia
Violet, the Major
London-pride, or None-so-pretty
Day-lily, red
Yellow
Fumitory, the yellow
White
Bulbous-rooted
American forked
Aconite, Monk's-hood, or Wolf's-bane
Blue Monk's-hood
Yellow
White
Wholesome Wolf's-bane
Winter Aconite
Hellebore, or Bear's-foot
Common black hellebore
Green-flowered
White Hellebore
Christmas Rose
Geranium, Crane's-bill
Bloody Crane's-bill
Blue
Roman
Bladder-cupped
Daisies, common double red garden daisy
White
Double variegated
Cock's-comb daisies, white and red
Hen and chicken, white and red
Dahlias, many varieties
Peony, double red
Double white

Double purple
Male, with large single flowers
Sweet-smelling Portugal
Double rose-colored
Silphium, bastard Chrysanthemum
Iris, Fleur-de-lis, or flags
The German violet-colored
Variegated, or Hungarian, purple and yellow
Chalcedonian iris
Greater Dalmatian iris
There are several other varieties of Irises, all very hardy and very beautiful plants
Cardinal Flowers, scarlet
Blue
Rocket, double white
Balm of Gilead, sweet-scented; must be sheltered in winter
Everlasting Pea
Eupatorium, several varieties
Eryngo, blue
White
Mountain, purple and violet
There are some other varieties
Snap Dragon, or Calf's-snout
Red
White
Variegated
Moth Mullein
Angelica
Asphodelus, King's-spear
Lupins, perennial, blue-flowered
Ononis, Rest-har
Large yellow-flowered
Tradescantia, or Virginia Spider-wort

The Saxifrage is propagated by cuttings and offsets, which the roots produce abundantly. Take the offsets and plant them out in August. The double white saxifrage is a beautiful flower, and blooms early in the spring. The pyramidal saxifrage is a very handsome decorative flower, but it must be planted in little clumps to make a showy appearance.

October is the busy month for transplanting and removing the offsets of all perennial and biennial plants. In this month every flower of summer has passed away, and the garden is free to receive all new arrangements in its future dispositions. Golden rod, Michaelmas daisies, everlasting sun-flower, and other branching plants, will require taking up every four years, to part the main root into separate plants, and replace them in the ground again. Peonies, lilies of the valley, fraxinellas, monk's-hood, flag-leaved irises, &c., must be increased or removed when required. All this is most effectually done in October.

In the same month, finish all that is to be effected among the perennial tribe. Campanulas, lychnises, polyanthuses, violets, aconites, cyclamens, gentianella, yellow gentian, double daisies, hepaticas, saxifrage, &c., must be attended to, and propagated, by dividing the roots, before October closes. November is the season of fogs and severe frosts: if a lady is prudent, she will perform all these needful operations in October, and November will have no alarms for her.

All the double-flowering plants, such as double sweet-william, double rockets, double scarlet lychnis, &c., should be placed in sheltered situations in October, to weather out the storms of winter. Double flowers are very handsome, and deserve a little care.

The most charming little perennial flower which can adorn a lady's garden is the scarlet verbena, but it is very difficult to preserve through the winter. Its beauty, however, repays the care which may be bestowed upon it. This tender plant—the only really tender root which I admit into my work—is not only desirable from its fine, full scarlet blossoms, but it blooms from April to November. The scarlet verbena loves a rich, light, dry border or bed, in a sunny situation; they delight also in rock-work, where they have been known to exist through the winter. Plant the roots about six inches apart in the middle of April, and keep pegging down the shoots as they throw themselves along the bed. A profusion of flowers and plants are produced by this means. A bed or border sloping to the south is the best situation for the scarlet verbena.

CHAPTER IV

BULBS AND TUBEROUS-ROOTED FLOWERS—PERENNIALS.

I SHALL give the bulbous and tuberous-rooted flowers a chapter to themselves. They are the earliest treasures of the flower-garden, and deserve especial notice. There was a period when two hundred pounds was offered for a hyacinth root, and even the enormous sum of six hundred pounds was given for a *Semper Augustus* tulip, by the Dutch tulip fanciers. But though a few florists are still particularly nice with respect to their bulbs, the time is past for paying such splendid prices; and such an inexhaustible variety offer themselves to our notice now, that we are somewhat puzzled in making a choice collection. Seed produces immense numbers yearly, and an infinite variety of new colors in each species. The florist is lost in admiration of the magnificent blooms which meet the eye in every flower-garden which is carefully attended to.

Bulbs love a mixture of garden soil and sand, well mixed, and dug about two spades deep to lighten it. Break the mould fine, and rake the surface even. Plant the bulbs four inches deep, and let them be six inches apart, placing the bulb with care into the dibbled hole, and pressing the earth gently round each. All bulbs should be replanted in September, and taken out of the ground when they have done flowering. When the leaves and stems decay, dig them neatly up, in dry weather, with your garden fork; take the offsets carefully from the main root; spread them out to dry on a mat, and put them in a cool dry place to plant again in September.

The common bulbs, such as *Snowdrops, Crocuses*, &c., may be left two or three years untouched; but at the end of that period take them up, to separate the offsets and small roots from the mother plants. You can replant them immediately, taking care to thin the clumps, and separate each root six inches from its neighbor, that they may rise healthy, and throw out fine blooms.

Narcissuses, Jonquils, and *Irises*, may also remain two years untouched; but if annually taken up, they will flower finer, and for these reasons.

By taking up your bulbs as soon as their leaves and stems decay, it not only allows you to separate the offsets, which weaken the parent bulb, but it prevents their receiving any damage from long drought, or the equally destructive moisture of heavy rains, which would set them growing again before their time, and exhaust them. The two or three months in which they are laid by contributes to their strength, by allowing them that period of complete rest.

The autumn-flowering bulbs, such as the *Colchicums*, the *Autumnal Crocus*, the *Yellow Autumnal Narcissus*, &c., should be aken up in May or early in June, when they are at rest. Translant them now, if you wish to remove them; part the offsets, id plant them six inches apart. If you keep them out of the ound, put them in a dry, shady place, till the middle of July August, when you must plant them again, to blow in the aunn.

Be careful to take up bulbs as soon as the leaves decay. If they are incautiously left in the ground beyond that period, they begin to form the bud for the next year's flowers; and the check of a removal would injure them. They might produce flowers in due time, but they would be weakly.

The little offsets will not flower for a year or two. They may be consigned to a nursery-bed to remain for that time, in order to swell and strengthen by themselves.

If you wish to procure new varieties from seed, it must be sown in August. The healthiest flower-stalk should be chosen, and deposited in pots or boxes of fine light earth, for the convenience of removing under shelter in wet or frost. Keep the pots or boxes in the shade during the heats, but, as the cold weather advances, remove them to a warm sheltered spot. Litter will shelter them from the frost, if you cannot command any other covering. The plants will appear early the following May: they must be kept very clear from weeds, and be moderately watered in dry weather. These seedlings must be transplanted every summer to be thinned, and placed further apart from each other till they blow, when they may be removed into the flower-beds.

This method is troublesome, and requires patience. Tulip seedlings are seven years before they flower, and a lady may find her patience severely tried in waiting for their blooms. Seven years is a large portion of human life. If you can persevere, however, you will be rewarded by beautiful varieties of new colors and stripes.

Fine tulips should have six leaves, three on the outside and three on the inside, and the former should be broader than the latter. The stripes upon the tulip should also be defined and distinct, not mixing with the ground tints.

Hyacinth seedlings are four years before they flower; this is not so harassing a period as the Tulip requires; but every pleasure has its counterbalance. If you will have fine flowers, you must wait for them. These bulbs love a sunny situation.

The *Orchis* tribe prefer a moist ground and a northern aspect. Columella says, that when orchis bulbs are sown in autumn, they germinate and bear flowers in April.

The *Colchicums* or narcissus are hardy bulbs, and will grow in any sort of ground; only, the better the soil is, the finer they will flower.

The *Guernsey Lily* and *Belladonna* will not thrive in the open ground, therefore it is needless to speak of those very splendid flowers.

The Lily of the Valley, though scarcely to be classed among the lily tribe, is a beautiful flower, and as fragrant as it is lovely. They must be multiplied by dividing the roots, which should be parted with a knife, as they are very intricate: do this in December. Plant them three inches deep in the ground, and disturb them as little as you can help, as they do not like to be often moved. They are larger in their flowers when grown in the shade, but they are sweeter in perfume in the sun's full rays. Thin broad leaves are sufficient shelter to the flowers.

All bulbs love salt: be careful, therefore, to throw a portion of common salt or brine upon your compost heap. My cousin, Cuthbert W. Johnson, Esq., in his "Observations on the Employment of Salt," quotes a passage in a letter addressed to him by Mr. Thomas Hogg, the eminent florist, upon the advantages of salt in the cultivation of flowers. I will transcribe it here:—

"From the few experiments that I have tried with salt as a garden manure, I am fully prepared to bear testimony to its usefulness. In a treatise upon flowers, published about six years since, I remarked, that the application of salt, and its utility as a manure, was yet imperfectly understood. It is a matter of uncertainty, whether it acts directly as a manure, or only as a kind of spice or seasoning, thereby rendering the soil a more palatable food for plants.

"The idea that first suggested itself to my mind, arose from contemplating the successful culture of hyacinths in Holland. This root, though not indigenous to the country, may be said to be completely naturalized in the neighborhood of Haerlem, where it grows luxuriantly in a deep, sandy, alluvial soil. yet one great cause of its free growth, I considered, was owing to the saline atmosphere this induced me to mix salt in the compost; and I am satisfied that no hyacinths will grow well at a distance from the sea without it. I am also of opinion, that the numerous bulbous tribe of Amaryllisses, especially those from the Cape of Good Hope; Ixias, Aliums, which include Onions, Garlic, Shalots, &c., Anemones, various species of the Lily Antholyza, Colchicum, Crinum, Cyclamens, Narcissus, Iris, Gladiolus, Ranunculus, Scilla, and many others, should either have salt or sea-sand in the mould used for them.

"I invariably use salt as an ingredient in my compost for carnations; a plant which, like wheat, requires substantial soil, and all the strength and heat of the summer, to bring it to perfection; and I believe I might say, without boasting, that few excel me in blooming that flower."

Colchicums, the Autumnal Narcissus, Amaryllis, and the Autumn Crocus, should be planted in August, to blow in September and October.

Replant all the bulbous tribe by the end of October, at the latest. Choose a mild, dry day to put them in the ground, and let each bulb be six or nine inches distant from its companion. All bulbs become weak by being placed too closely together, the soil becoming soon exhausted.

Bulbs of the more choice varieties are better attended to if they can be placed in beds or compartments by themselves; for they are more easily sheltered from frost and rain when in a body. The eye, also, is more delighted by the beautiful variety *en masse.* Their favorite soil, too, can be composed and preserved for them more exclusively, unexhausted by the roots of larger plants around them. Some of the commoner sorts can be planted out in patches, to add to the gay appearance of the borders, among the spring flowers.

Martagons, orange lilies, and bulbs, of tall growth, should never be planted among the smaller tribe; their large bulbs would exhaust the soil, and weaken the smaller flowers. They look very handsome in borders and plots, placed near, or in, their center.

LIST OF BULBOUS AND TUBEROUS-ROOTED FLOWERS.

Amaryllis, comprising the autumnal yellow Narcissus
Spring ditto
Crocus vernus, or spring-flowering crocus
Common yellow
Large yellow
Yellow, with black stripes
White
White, with blue stripes
Blue, with white stripes
Deep blue
Light blue
White, with purple bottom
Scotch, or black and white striped
Cream-colored
Autumnal flowering Crocus, of the following varieties:—
True saffron crocus, with bluish flower, and golden stigma, which is the saffron
Common autumnal crocus, with deep blue flowers
With light blue flowers
Many-flowered
Snowdrop, the small spring flowering
Common single
Double
Leucojum, or great summer snowdrop
Great summer snowdrop with angular stalk: a foot high, and two or three flowers in each sheath
Taller great snowdrop, with many flowers
Ornithogalum, or Star of Bethlehem
Great white pyramidal, with narrow leaves
White, with broadsword-shaped leaves spreading on the ground
Yellow
Pyrenean, with whitish green flowers
Star of Naples, with hanging flowers
Umbellated, producing its flowers in umbels, or spreading bunches, at the top of the stalk
Low yr low umbellated
Erythronium, lens canis, or dog's tooth
Round-leaved, with red flowers
Same, with white flowers
The same, yellow
Long narrow-leaved, with purple and with white flowers
Grape hyacinth
Purple
Blue
White
Musk hyacinth
White
Ash-colored
Blue feathered hyacinth
Purple
Musky, or sweet-scented, with full purple flowers
The same, with large purple and yellow flowers
Great African Muscaria, with sulphur-colored flower
Fritillaria checkered tulip
Early purple, variegated, or checkered with white
Black, checkered with yellow spots
Yellow, checkered with purple
Dark purple, with yellow spots, and flowers growing in an umbel
Persian lily, with tall stalks, and dark purple flowers growing in a pyramid
Branching Persian lily
Corona Imperialis, crown imperial, a species of Fritillaria
Common red
Common yellow
Yellow-striped
Sulphur-colored
Large-flowering
Double of each variety
Crown upon crown, or with two whorls of flowers
Triple crown upon crown, or with three tiers of flowers one above another
Gold-striped leaved
Silver-striped leaved

Tulip, early dwarf tulip
Tall, or most common tulip
Early, yellow and red striped
White and red striped
White and purple striped
White and rose striped
Tall, or late-flowering, with white bottoms, striped with brown
White bottoms, striped with violet or black brown
White bottoms, striped with red or vermilion
Yellow bottoms, striped with different colors, called Bizarres
Double Tulip, yellow and red
White and red
Gladiolus, corn flag, or sword lily, common, with sword-shaped leaves, and a reddish purple flower ranged on one side of the stalk
The same, with white flowers
Italian with reddish flowers ranged on both sides of the stalk
The same, with white flowers
Great red of Byzantium
Narrow grassy-leaved, and a flesh-colored flower, with channeled, long, narrow, four-angled leaves, and two bell-shaped flowers on the stalk
Great Indian
Anemone, wood anemone, with blue flowers
White flowers
Red flowers
Double white
Garden Double Anemone, with crimson flowers
Purple
Red
Blue
White
Red and white striped
Red, white, and purple
Rose and white
Blue, striped with white
Ranunculus, Turkey with a single stalk, and large double bloo·-red flower
Yellow-flowered
Persian, with branching stalk, and large double flowers of innumerable varieties, of which there are
Very double flowers
Semi, or half double
(The double are most beautiful, propagated by offsets)
Pancratium, sea daffodil
Common white sea Narcissus, with many flowers in a sheath, and tongue-shaped leaves
Sclavonian, with taller stems and many white flowers, and sword-shaped leaves
Broad-leaved American, with large white flowers, eight or ten in a sheath
Mexican, with two flowers
Ceylon, with one flower
Moly (*Allium*), species of garlic producing flowers
Broad-leaved yellow
Great broad-leaved, with lily flowers
Broad-leaved, with white flowers in large round umbels
Smaller white umbellated
Purple
Rose-colored
Fumaria bulbosa, or bulbous-rooted fumitory
Greater purple
Hollow-rooted
American, with a forked flower
Narcissus, or daffodil, common double yellow daffodil
Single yellow, with the middle cup as long as the petals
White, with yellow cups
Double, with several cups, one within another
Common white narcissus, with single flowers
Double white narcissus
Incomparable, or great nonsuch, with double flowers
With single flowers
Hoop petticoat narcissus, or rush-leaved daffodil, with the middle cup larger than the petals, and very broad at the brim

Daffodil, with white reflexed petals, and golden cups
White daffodil, with purple cups
Polyanthus Narcissus, having many small flowers on a stalk, from the same sheath. Of this are the following varieties :—
White, with white cups
Yellow, with yellow cups
White, with yellow cups
White, with orange cups
White, with sulphur-colored cups
Yellow, with orange cups
Yellow, with sulphur-colored cups
With several intermediate varieties
Autumnal narcissus
quil, common single
Large single
Common double
Double, with large round roots
lium, the lily, common white lily
With spotted or striped flowers
With double flowers
With striped leaves
White lily, with hanging or pendent flowers
Common orange lily, with large single flowers
With double flowers
With striped leaves
Fiery, bulb-bearing lily, producing bulbs at the joints of the stalks
Common narrow-leaved
Great broad-leaved
Many-flowered
Hoary
Martagon lily, sometimes called Turk's-cap, from the reflexed position of their flower-leaves. There are many varieties, and which differ from the other sorts of lilies in having the petals of their flowers reflexed, or turned backward. The varieties are—
Common red martagon, with very narrow sparsed leaves, or such as grow without order all over the flower-stalk
Double martagon
White
Double white
White spotted
Scarlet, with broad sparsed leaves
Bright red, many-flowered, or pompony, with short, grassy, sparsed leaves
Reddish hairy martagon, with leaves growing in whorls round the stalk
Great yellow, with pyramidal flowers, spotted
Purple, with dark spots, and broad leaves in whorls round the stalk, or most common Turk's-cap
White spotted Turk's-cap
Canada martagon, with yellowish large flowers spotted, and leaves in whorls
Campscatense martagon, with erect bell-shaped flowers
Philadelphia martagon, with two erect bright purple flowers
Squills, sea onion, or lily hyacinth, common lily hyacinth, with a lily root and blue flower
Peruvian, or broad-leaved hyacinth of Peru, with blue flowers
With white flowers
Early white starry hyacinth
Blue
Autumnal starry hyacinth
Larger starry blue hyacinth of Byzantium
Purple star-flower of Peru
Italian blue-spiked star-flower
Asphodel lily, African blue, with a tuberous root
Tuberose, or Indian tuberous hyacinth. It produces a small stem three or four feet high, adorned with many white flowers of great fragrance.
The varieties are,—
Fine double tuberose
Single tuberose
Small-flowered
Striped-leaved
Iris bulbosa, or bulbous Iris, Persian with three erect blue petals called standards, and three reflexed petals called falls, which

are variegated, called Persian bulbous iris, with a variegated flower
Common narrow-leaved bulbous iris, with a blue flower
White
Yellow
Blue, with white falls
Blue, with yellow falls
Greater broad-leaved bulbous iris, with a deep blue flower
Bright purple
Deep purple
Variegated
Great, with broad and almost plain or flat leaves, with blue flowers
Purple
Of the above there are many intermediate varieties

Hyacinth, eastern, with large flowers. Of these there are many varieties, and of which there are innumerable intermediate shades or tints of color

Of double sorts there are,—
Blues
Purple blues
Agatha blues
Whites
Whites, with yellow eyes
Whites, with red eyes
Whites, with violet or purple eyes
Whites, with rose-colored eyes
Whites, with scarlet eyes
Reds
Incarnate, flesh or rose-colored

Of single sorts there are,—
Blues, of various shades, as above
Whites
Reds
Rose-colored
With many intermediate shades or varieties

(*Muscaria*), or musk hyacinth
Ash-colored
White
Obsolete purple
Greater yellow African
Grape hyacinth
Purple
Blue
White
Red
Monstrous flowering, or blue-feathered hyacinth
Comosed, or tufted purple hyacinth
Amethystine blue hyacinth
Nodding, spiked, red hyacinth
Non-script small English hyacinth, or harebells, of the following varieties:—
Common blue flowers arranged on one side of the stalk
White
Bell-shaped blue hyacinth, with flowers on every side of the stalk
Bell-shaped peach-colored, with flowers on one side of the stalk
These are very hardy, propagating by offsets
Hyacinth, with a pale purple flower

Colchicums in variety

Leontice, lion's leaf, largest yellow with single foot-stalks to the leaves
Smaller pale yellow, with branched foot-stalks to the leaves

Cyclamen, sow-bread, European, or common autumn-flowering, with a purple flower, and angular heart-shaped leaves
The same, with a black flower
The same, with white flowers
Red spring-flowering, with heart-shaped leaves, marbled with white
Entire white, sweet-smelling
Purple winter-flowering, with plain or circular shining green leaves
Purple round-leaved autumn-flowering
Small, or anemone-rooted, with flesh-colored flowers appearing in autumn: these plants have large, round, solid roots; the flowers and leaves rise immediately from the root

Corona Regalis, or royal crown; requires shelter in the winter	*Aconite*, the winter *Sisyrinchium*

AURICULA, RANUNCULUS, ANEMONE.

These early and beautiful flowers deserve peculiar notice, for no garden looks well without them, and their bright tints delight the eye and mind. The commonest kinds are handsome and useful in small clumps, and a little care and trouble will raise superb varieties.

The Auricula loves a soil composed of kitchen-garden mould, sand, and cow-dung, well mixed together; they also like a cool situation. The seed should be sown in September, and when sown give it a gentle watering. By sowing the seed in pots or boxes, you can remove them from heavy rains, &c., without trouble, and shelter them in the outhouses or tool-house. The seed seldom appears under six months, and it has been sometimes a twelvemonth producing itself, therefore be not in despair, but remain patient; these freaks of nature cannot be accounted for. When they flower, you must single out the plants which bear the finest and most choice blooms, and transplant them into pots filled with the compost above described. The common sorts may be planted in the borders, to remain out and shift for themselves. By keeping the fine auriculas in pots, you preserve them through the winter easily, for heavy rains and cutting winds do them harm. You can sink them in their pots during summer in the flower-beds, but let them be sheltered during the winter, if you wish to preserve the blooms uninjured.

Auriculas multiply also by suckers, which grow on their roots. Take off these in February, and plunge them into pots of the mould they like best, to root freely. They will do so in two months. Auriculas should not be too much watered, as it makes them look sickly, and the leaves become yellow. When you pot the auriculas, sink them up to their leaves in the soil, but do not press the mould round the plant, as the flowers bloom finest when the roots touch the sides of the flower pot.

The auricula is esteemed fine that has a low stem, a stalk proportioned to the flower, the eye well opened, and always dry. The glossy, the velvet, and the streaked auriculas are the most admired. The stalk should be decked with many flower-bells, to be handsome and healthy.

Take care to pull off all dead leaves round the plant at all times, that it may appear neat and clean. Neatness is favorable to its perfect growth, as well as decorating it to the eye.

The Ranunculus does not like being mixed up with other flowers, and from this "aristocratic principle" it is always planted in separate knots

This flower loves sun and warmth. The root must be planted in September, to bloom early in the summer, and it delights in a rich, moist soil, well dug, and raked soft and fine. When you plant them in beds or pots, they must be sunk two inches deep, and dibble the hole with a round, not pointed, dibble. Place the roots four or five inches apart, in the warmest situation in your garden. By planting ranunculuses in pots, you can more easily place them in warm situations, and withdraw them from heavy rains. The more room you give these roots the finer they will grow and blow. If your plots will allow of so doing, let the roots be planted six or seven inches apart. The flowers will repay your care. When ranunculuses in pots have flowered, remove them from the August rains, or take up the roots, to replant in September.

The Ranunculus with the double white flower must not be taken up until September, when it should be taken up quickly, its roots parted, and replanted immediately

The Yellow Ranunculus with the rue leaf, prefers being potted to being planted in beds.

The Ranunculus propagates by seed as well as offsets. Sow the seed as you do that of the auricula.

The most admired ranunculuses are the white, the golden yellow, the pale yellow, the citron-colored, and the brown red. The red is the least esteemed. The yellow ranunculus speckled with red, is handsome,—also the rose-color with white inside.

Great varieties are obtained by seed.

The Anemones love a light soil, composed of kitchen-garden mould, and sand, and leaf mould, well mixed, and sifted fine. It should, if possible, be composed a year before it is used; the lighter it is the better for anemones.

The seed should be sown in September. The single flowers alone bear seed, which is fit to gather when it appears ready to fly away with the first gust of wind. As soon as the seed is lodged, and raked smoothly into its fine, light bed, strew the bed over with straw or matting, and give it a good watering. In three weeks the seed will begin to rise, when the straw may be removed. The young plants will flower in the following April.

When the roots are to be planted in September, sink them about three inches deep, and six inches apart, that they may come up strong and flower well. Make a hole in the ground for them with your finger, and set them upon the broadest side, with the slit downwards.

Those anemones planted in September will flower in March and April, and the roots planted in May flower in autumn, but the flowers are never so fine.

When anemones have done flowering, it requires some care in taking up the roots, in order to part and put them by till the time for replanting arrives. The roots or flaps are so small and difficult to distinguish, that the earth should be taken up and laid upon a sieve to be sifted, when the flaps will alone remain behind, or the earth may be deposited upon an open newspaper or cloth, and well rubbed with the hand to feel for the minute dark-colored flaps, which may easily escape observation.

The beauty of this flower consists in its thickness and roundness, especially when the great leaves are a little above the thickness of the tuft.

Choose your seed from the finest single anemone, with a broad, round leaf.

The remaining tuberous-rooted flowers are very hardy.

BIENNIALS.

Biennial flowers, as the name implies, are plants that exist only two years. They are propagated by seed, rising the first year, and flowering the second. If they continue another year, they are sickly and languid. The double biennials may be continued by cuttings and slips of the tops, as well as by layers and pipings, though the parent flower dies—but they are not so fine. A lady should have a space of ground allotted to biennial seedlings, so that a fresh succession of plants may be ready to supply the place of those which die away. The seeds should be sown every spring in light, well-dug earth; the young plants should be kept very clean, and some inches apart from each other; and they must be finally transplanted in autumn into the beds where they are intended to remain.

But there is a great uncertainty as to raising the double flowers, therefore it is better to make sure of those you approve by perpetuating them as long as you can, by any root offsets they may throw off,—by pipings, cuttings, or by layers, as before noticed I subjoin a list of the principal and useful biennials.

LIST OF HARDY BIENNIALS.

Canterbury Bells
Blue-flowers
White
Purple
Pyramidal
Carnation. All the varieties, somewhat biennial-perennial.
Clary, Purple topped
Red-topped
Colutea, Æthiopian
French Honeysuckle
Red
White
Globe Thistle
Hollyhocks. Somewhat biennial-perennial; all the varieties; always by seed
Lunaria, Moonwort or Honesty
Mallow (Tree)
Red
Scarlet
Purple
Red, white-bordered
Party-colored
Variegated
Painted Lady
Double of each
Mule, or Mongrel Sweet-william, or Mule Pink
Tree Mallow (*Lavatera arborea*)
Tree Primrose
Night Stock
Poppy, Yellow-horned (*Chelidonium glaucum*)
Rocket, Dame's violet
Single white
Double white
Double purple
Single purple
Rose Campion
Red
White
Scabius, double
Dark purple-flowered
Dark-red
White
Starry purple-flowered
Starry white
Jagged-leaved starry
Stock Gilliflower
Brompton
Queen
Twickenham
Sweet-william
Common upright tall yellow
Small-flowered
Wall-flower
Yellow-flowered
Bloody
White
Double of each
Petunia
White
Lilac

When you make your seedling-bed or nursery, cover it over with straw, or fern, or matting, during frost; and to prevent the birds pecking up the seeds, it is requisite to protect the bed by strewing light boughs of thorn bushes over it, or fixing a net upon sticks as a covering, till the plants appear. If cats, dogs or poultry intrude into the flower garden, it is in vain to hope for enjoyment.

Sow your biennial seeds in March, April, or May. I recommend May, because the young plants in that month germ and vegetate quickly, surely, and without requiring defenses from the frost. Plant them out in October, with a ball of earth to each root, where they are to remain.

The Stock Gilliflowers in particular, having long, naked roots, must be planted out very young, otherwise they do not succeed well.

Honesty is a very early, rich-flowering biennial, which requires no care; they shed their seed, rise, and flower without any assistance, in profusion. The only trouble is to weed it out of the beds, that they may not stand in the way of other flowers.

Canterbury Bells are handsome flowers, and will bloom a long time, if you cut off the bells as they decay.

The deep crimson Sweet-williams are most esteemed; though every variety looks well.

Sweet-williams may be increased by layers and cuttings, which is the only sure way of securing the sorts you like; for you may sow seed every year, and not one in a thousand will reward you by coming up double.

Carnations are the pride of a garden, and deserve great care and attention. The common sorts, which are planted in borders, should have a good rich earth about them, and be treated like the pink; but the finer sorts should always be potted, to protect and shelter the plant from hares, rabbits, heavy rains, and severe frost in the winter. Refresh the top of the pots with new soil in June, and keep the plants free from decayed leaves. Gently stir the earth round each plant occasionally; and as plants in pots require more water than if placed in the ground, let the carnations be gently moistened about every other day during dry weather. Let the watering take place in the *evening;* no flower will endure being watered during the heat of a summer's day. Carnations love sand and salt in proper proportions. The brine which is deposited upon the compost heap will answer every purpose of salts, (if it be regularly carried out), without adding common salt: but let this be particularly attended to. The cook should deposit her pickle and brine to good purpose upon the compost heap, instead of splashing it down in front of her kitchen door.

Let each plant be well staked, and neatly tied to its supporter; and do not allow two buds to grow side by side upon the same stem, for one will weaken the other. Pinch off the smaller bud. Carnations love warmth; therefore give them a sunny aspect to blow in. The seedling plants may be treated like young pinks, but this difference must be observed—pinks love shade, and carnations love warmth. A bed of carnations is a beautiful object. The pots can always be sunk in a border or bed in fine weather. Carnations may be layered, or piped, or slipped for propagation.

Water your carnations in pots once a week with lime water, if they appear drooping, for this proceeds from a worm at the root; but the brine will destroy all insects quickly, when poured upon the compost heap.

In propagating double Wall-flowers, take slips of the young shoots of the head: this will perpetuate the double property and color of the flower, from which they were slipped. In saving seed for wall-flowers, choose the single flowers, which have five petals or flower leaves. Double flowers have no seed.

Water the slips, and keep them shady and moist: they will root by September.

Plant your Hollyhocks in September or October, where they are to remain. Hollyhocks are a noble flower, and they love a strong soil. Let a succession of these flower plants be attended to in the biennial seed-bed. Keep them some inches apart from each other in the seedling-bed, for they form large straggling roots. The hollyhock looks well in clumps of three, at a good distance apart, in large gardens or shrubberies, but they are somewhat too overgrown for smaller parterres.

Be particular in gathering your seeds on a fine, dry day, and put each sort in a separate brown paper bag till you require them. The very finest seedlings are, after all, those which spring near the mother plant from self-sown seed, therefore, when you weed or dig your flower borders, be careful not to disturb any seedlings which may have sprung up. They always make strong, fine blooming plants.

Take care of your double-flowering plants in winter. The double wall-flower is hardy enough to exist in the borders, but the other double biennials deserve to be sheltered, for double flowers are very handsome, and heavy rains, snow, or severe frost, injures them. Take cuttings every year from them.

The Night Stock is tolerably hardy if sheltered during the frost by ashes or litter. The sweetness after night-fall must recommend it to all the lovers of fragrant flowers.

PROPAGATING BIENNIALS.

Every young lady must become acquainted with the manner of operating upon plants, to preserve the finer sorts, which they may wish to perpetuate. Raising from seed is slow, but it produces infinite variety. You, however, rarely see the same flower produced twice from seed; therefore you must propagate the biennial and perennial flowers by layers, slips, pipings, and cuttings, if you wish to preserve any particular sorts.

To effect layers, prepare some rich, light earth, a parcel of small hooked sticks, or little pegs, and a sharp penknife.

Now clear the ground about the plant you are going to layer; stir the surface well with your trowel, and put a sufficient quantity of the prepared mould round the plant as will raise the surface to a convenient height for receiving the layer.

Cut off the top of each shoot with your knife, about two inches, and pull off the lower leaves; then fix upon a joint about the middle of the shoot, and, placing your knife under it, *slit* the shoot from that joint, rather more than half way up, towards the joint above it.

Now make an opening in the earth, and lay the stem, and slit or gashed shoot, into it, and peg it down; taking care to raise the head of the shoot as upright as you can, that it may grow shapely; then cover it with the new mould, and press the mould gently round it. Do this by each shoot till the plant is layered—that is, till every shoot is laid down. They must be watered often in dry weather, but moderately, not to disturb or wash away the soil round the layers. In six weeks' time, each gashed or slit shoot will have rooted, and become a distinct plant. They may be taken away from the old parent stem in September, and dug up with a ball of earth round each root, to be transplanted into the plots or borders where they are to remain.

Carnations, pinks, sweet-williams, double wall-flowers, &c., are the flowers most deserving of layers.

Piping, which belongs almost exclusively to carnations and pinks, is a most expeditious mode of raising young plants.

Take off the upper and young part of each shoot, close below a joint, with a sharp knife, and cut each off at the third joint, or little knob; then cut the top leaves down pretty short, and take off the lower and discolored ones. When you have piped in this way as many as you require, let them stand a week in a tumbler of water, which greatly facilitates their doing well. Indeed, I never failed in any pipings, slips, or cuttings, which I allowed to soak and swell in water previous to planting. When you plant the pipings, let the ground be nicely dug, and raked very fine; dibble no hole, but gently thrust each piping half way down into the soft earth, slightly pressing the earth round each, to fix it in the bed. Water them often if the weather is dry, but moderately, just to keep them moist; and shade them from the hot sun in the day. If pipings are covered with a hand-glass, they root earlier, by three weeks, than those which are exposed.

Laying, piping, and slipping, are done in June and July. The plants will be well rooted, and fit to plant out, in October.

The operation of slipping is easy. Tear the top shoots of the plant to be so propagated, gently from their sockets; hold the shoot between your finger and thumb, as near the socket as you can, and it will tear as easily and neatly as you carve the wing of poultry or game. Place the slips in water for a few days previous to planting them, like pipings. They will root in six weeks or two months, if kept shady and moist.

Cuttings must be made of shoots of the last year's growth of roses, honeysuckles, &c., and planted in February. Choose the strong shoots, and do not cut them less than six inches long. Cut them with your knife in a slanting direction. Plant them in a shady place, each cutting half way in the ground, which should be cleaned, and well dug and raked, to receive them. Cuttings made in February will root well by October.

Cuttings of flower stalks, such as scarlet lychnis, should be done in May, June, and July. Take cuttings from the youngest flower stems, and plant them carefully in nice mould, like pipings. These flower cuttings should be in lengths of four joints each. Covering them with a hand-glass raises them very quickly. They root in two months.

Where hand-glasses are not to form any part of a lady's arrangements, oil-papered frames are equally useful. I have seen very economical and useful frames made of bamboo, in the *form* of hand-glasses, covered neatly with glazed white cotton or linen, or horn paper, made by a lady with great celerity and ingenuity; and her cuttings and pipings succeeded under them admirably. Whatever shelters cuttings and pipings from the rays of the sun effects a material purpose. Linen is the best shelter in the world from heat, but oiled or horn paper resists rain better.

Dr. Priestley is of opinion that salt water is very efficacious for cuttings, if they are placed in it for a few days previous to planting. He remarks that it is a custom with the importers of exotic plants to dip cuttings in salt and water, otherwise they would perish on the passage.

CHAPTER V.

ANNUALS.

ANNUALS, as I have observed before, are flowers that rise, bloom, and die in the same year; and must therefore be raised from seed every year.

The first class of annuals, being very delicate, and requiring great care, with the constant assistance of glass frames, I shall not even name, since they do not enter into the nature of my work.

I proceed to the second class, which are hardier than the above, though they should be raised in a warm border, and be covered with a hand-glass, if you wish them to flower in good time.

The ten weeks' Stocks will grow, if sown in a warm border, towards the end of March, and should be afterwards transplanted; but if brought up in a hot-bed, they will flower a month or six weeks earlier.

The China-aster, Chrysanthemum, white and purple Sultan, African and French Marigolds, Persicarias, &c., will grow well in a warm border of natural earth, if sown in April; but they also flower a month earlier if they are assisted by a hot-bed or glass. These annuals must be all planted out when tolerably strong, into the spots where they are destined to remain in the borders, taking care to allow to each plant plenty of space, that they may not crowd each other. The China-aster branches into many stems and flowers, therefore they may be planted singly, or not less than six inches apart. The July flowers, or more commonly called gilliflowers, become expansive as they increase. They should not be crowded together; three in a group are quite sufficient, and they should be six inches apart. The same may be said of the stock varieties.

I have ever found the hardy annuals grow finest by allowing them to become self-sown. They flower some weeks earlier, and invariably produce larger and brighter flowers.

When gathering my flower seeds in August and September, I allow one half to remain sprinkled over the borders; and the young plants never fail appearing healthy and strong above ground in March and April, the months appropriated to sowing the seed. Thus, my Lavateras, Larkspurs, &c., are in beautiful blow, while the second crop, or seeds sown in spring, are but showing their green heads above the surface. I weed away the superfluous self-sown plants to my taste; but the birds take care that no one shall be encumbered with a superfluity. I have by this means a first and second crop of the same annuals, but the crop of self-sown are far superior. They are up before the heats come on, to dry the earth, and dwindle the flower.

Dig the ground well with your trowel, and rake it very fine, before you put in the seeds in spring. Annuals love a light, friable soil. All the hardy kinds may be sown in March, each sort in little separate patches, as follows:—

Draw a little earth off the top to one side, then sprinkle in the seed, not too plentifully, and cover it again with the drawn-off earth. Half an inch is sufficient depth for small seed. The larger kind, such as sweet-peas, lupins, &c., must be sown an inch in depth. When the plants have been up some time, thin them well. The more space you have, the finer the plants will rise.

The hardy annuals will not bear transplanting: they must be

left to flourish where they are sown. The large kinds, such as the lavatera or mallow, should only be sown in groups of three plants together. The lupin tribe should not exceed five plants in a group. The Convolvulus, also, requires four or five plants only in a group. Water the patches in dry weather moderately, and be careful never to use pump water. If you have no soft water, a tub should be placed in the garden to receive rain water; and if, as in towns, pump water must be chiefly used, let it remain a day or two in the tub, to soften in the air and sunshine.

The first week in April is the safest period for sowing annuals, as the cutting winds have ceased by that time, and frost is not so much to be apprehended. The soft rains, also, fall in warm showers, to give life and germ to seeds and plants, and they appear in a shorter space of time.

Those ladies who live in the vicinity of nursery gardens have a great advantage over the more remote flower-fanciers. They can be supplied, at a trifling expense, with all the tender annuals from hot-beds, either in pots, or drawn ready for immediate transplanting.

If you do not raise your own seed, be careful how you purchase your stock, and of whom you receive it. Many seedsmen sell the refuse of many years' stock to their youthful customers, and produce great disappointment. There is one way of ascertaining the goodness of the seed, which will not deceive. Previous to sowing, plunge your lupin, sunflower, &c., seeds into a tumbler of water: the good seed will sink, while the light and useless part remains floating on the surface.

If you grow your own seed, exchange it every two years with your neighbors. Seeds love change of soil: they degenerate, if repeatedly grown and sown upon the same spot, particularly sweet-peas.

Sweet-peas should be put into the ground early in March, for they will bear the wind and weather. Make a circle round a pole, or some object to which they may cling as they rise; and put the peas an inch deep, having soaked them previously in water well saturated with arsenic, to guard them from the depredations of birds and mice. Add an outer circle of peas every month, so that a continual bloom may appear. The circle first sown will ripen and pod for seed in the center, while the outer vines will continue flowering till late in the autumn. When you have gathered a sufficient number of ripe pods, cut away all the pods which may afterwards form with your knife. This strengthens the vines, and throws all their vigor into repeated blooms.

Be very careful to throw away the arsenic water upon your heap of compost, and do not put that powerful poison into any thing which may be used afterwards in the house. Soak the peas in a flower-pot saucer which is never required for any other purpose, and keep it on a shelf in the tool-house, covered up. Three or four hours' soaking will be sufficient. If the wind and frosts be powerful and continued, shelter the peas through March, by covering them with straw or matting every evening.

I have got sweet-peas into very early blow by bringing them up in pots in-doors, and transplanting them carefully in April, without disturbing the roots. In doing this, push your finger gently through the orifice at the bottom of the flower-pot, and raise its contents "bodily." Then place the ball of earth and plants into a hole troweled out to receive it; cover it round gently, and, if the weather is dry, water it moderately.

Ten-weeks' Stock is a very pretty annual, and continues a long time in bloom. Mignionette is the sweetest of all perfumes, and should be sown in September for early blowing, and again in March for a later crop. It is always more perfumy and healthy, if dug into the ground in autumn to sow itself. Venus' Looking-glass is a very pretty, delicate flower. Indeed, every annual is lovely; and the different varieties give a gay and rich appearance to the flower garden during the three summer months.

The Clarkias are very pretty annuals, with a hundred other varieties lately introduced, and which are all specified in Mrs. Loudon's new work upon annuals. My plan is, to give a general idea of their treatment only, under the classification of hardy annuals, or those annuals which may be nurtured without a hot-bed.

Keep your annuals from looking wild and disorderly in a garden by allotting the smaller kinds their separate patches of ground; and trim the larger annuals from branching among other flowers. For instance, cut away the lower branches of the China-aster, the African marigold, &c., and train the plant erect and neatly to a slight rod or stick; cut away the flowers as they droop, reserving one or two of the finest blooms only for seed: and let each plant look clean and neat in its own order. By cutting away flowers as they droop, the plant retains vigor enough to continue throwing out fresh flowers for a long period.

SECOND, OR LESS TENDER CLASS OF ANNUALS.

African Marigold, the orange
Yellow
Straw-colored
Double of each
Double-quilled
French Marigold, the striped
The yellow
Sweet-scented
China-aster, the double
Double purple
Double white
Double-striped
Marvel of Peru, the red striped
Yellow-striped
Long-tubed
Chrysanthemum, the double white
Double yellow
Double-quilled
Sweet Sultan, the yellow
White
Red
Indian Pink, double
Single
Large imperial
Alkekengi
Palma Christi, the common
Tall red-stalked
Smaller green-leaved
Smallest
Tobacco, long-leaved Virginia
Broad-leaved
Branching perennial
Love Apple, with red fruit
With yellow fruit
Gourds, the round smooth orange
Rock, or warted
Pear-shaped yellow
Pear-shaped striped

Stone colored
Bottle Gourd, some very large, from two or three to five or six feet long, and of various shapes
Momordica Balsamina
Persicaria
Indian Corn, the tall Dwarf
Nolana prostrata, blue
Convolvulus, scarlet-flowered
Yellow Balsam, or Touch-me-not
Capsicum, long red-podded
Long yellow-podded
Red, short, thick, roundish podded
With heart-shaped pods
With cherry-shaped fruit, red
Cherry-shaped fruit, yellow
Basil, the common, or sweet-scented
Bush basil
Zinnia, red
Yellow
Amaranthus
Tree Amaranthus
Prince's feather amaranthus
Love-lies-bleeding amaranthus
Cannacorus, yellow
Red
Chinese Hollyhock, the variegated
Ten-week Stock Gilliflower
The double red
Double white
Double purple
White Ten-week Stock, with a wall-flower leaf
With double and single flowers
The double of this sort makes a pretty appearance

The following are hardy annuals, requiring no assistance of artificial heat, but should all be sown in the place where it is designed they shall flower:—

Adonis Flower, or Flos Adonis, the red-flowering
The yellow
Candytuft, the large
Purple
White
Larkspur, the double rose
Double-branched
Large double blue
Double white
Lupins, the rose
Large blue
Small blue
Yellow
White
Scarlet
Marbled
Sunflower, the tall double
Double dwarf
Lavatera, red
White
Poppy, the double tall striped carnation
Dwarf-striped
Double corn poppy
Horned poppy
Convolvulus, major
Minor
Striped
White
Scarlet
Ketmia bladder
Starry Scabius
Hawkweed, the yellow
Purple, or red
Spanish
Carthamus tinctorius, or saffron flower
Nasturtium, the large
Small
Cerinthe major, or great Honey-wort
Tangier Pea
Sweet Pea, the painted lady
The purple
White
Scarlet
Winged Pea
Crowned Pea
Nigella, or devil in a bush, the long blue, or Spanish
The white
Oriental mallow, curled

Venetian mallow
Lobel's Catchfly, white and red
Arbiscus
Pimpernel
Dwarf Lychnis
Venus's Navel-wort
Venus's Looking-glass
Virginian Stock
Strawberry Spinach
Noli me tangere, or Touch-me-not
Heart's Ease
Snail Plant
Large ditto
Caterpillar Plant
Hedgehog Plant
Antirrhinum, snap-dragon, the annual
Nolana, blue
Cyanus, or corn-bottle, the red
White
Blue
Roman Nettle
Belvidere, or summer cypress
Garden, or *common*, *Marigold*, the common single
Double orange
Double lemon-colored
Double lemon-colored ranunculus marigold
Annual Cape Marigold, with a violet and white flower
Mignionette, or reseda, the sweet-scented
The upright
Xeranthemum, or eternal flower, red and white
Purple Clary
Purple Jacobæa
Dracocephalum, the purple
Blue
Capnoides, or bastard fumitory
Ten-week Stock Gilliflowers, in variety
Persicaria
Tobacco Plant
Long-leaved,
Round-leaved
Indian Corn
Amethystea
Globe Thistle
Clarkias

CHAPTER VI.

ROSES AND JASMINES.

THESE most delicious, most elegant flowers—in themselves a garden—are worthy of a chapter devoted exclusively to their culture. What cottage exists without its roses twined around the doorway, or blooming up its pathway? What is sentiment without its roses? What other flower illustrates the beauty and excellence of a loved one?—

> "Oh! my love is like the red, red rose,
> That sweetly blows in June."

Every gentle feeling, every exquisite thought, every delicate allusion, is embodied in the rose. It is absurd to say the rose by any other name "would smell as sweet." It is not so. Poetry, painting, and music, have deified the rose. Call it "nettle," and we should cast it from our hands in disgust.

There are innumerable varieties of roses, from the cottage rose to the fairy rose, whose buds are scarcely so large as the bells of the lily of the valley. Mrs. Gore mentions some hundreds of sorts, but such a catalogue is too mighty to insert in my little work. I will name only the well-known hardy kinds, and refer my reader to Mrs. Gore herself for the complete collection. Seed yields such inexhaustible varieties, that a new list will be required every ten years.

The *Damask rose* is very useful from its properties, as well as its beauty and hardihood. Rose-water is distilled from this bright, thickly-blowing flower

The *Cabbage roses* is the most beautiful, as well as the most fragrant of roses. All others are varieties of roses, but this grand flower is the "rose itself."

It throws out suckers plentifully for propagating its kind; and every two or three years, the root of each bush will part into separate plants. Cut the roots slanting with a sharp knife as you divide them. A very small bit of root is sufficient for a rose-bush, as they are hardy in their nature. Do not move roses oftener than you can help: they delight in being stationary for years.

In pruning roses of every description, which should be effected in January, shorten all the shoots to nine inches only, and cut away all the old wood, which becomes useless after two or three years' growth. This treatment insures fine flowers.

Roses love a good soil, as, indeed, what flower does not? Fresh mould applied to them every two or three years, or manure dug round them annually, preserves them in constant vigor and beauty.

Shoots of rose-bushes laid down and pegged like layers, only without gashing, when the flowers are in bloom, will root and become plants in the autumn. Pinch off their buds, that they may throw their strength into their roots.

Roses are often observed to change their color, which effect proceeds chiefly from bad soil. When this occurs, manure the root of the bush or plant. A clay soil, well dressed with ashes, is the best of all soils for the hardy roses.

Moss roses love a cool soil and a cool aspect. They soon fade in a hot sun.

A pyramid of climbing roses is a beautiful object in a garden. Iron or wooden stakes, twelve feet in height, gradually approaching each other, till they meet at the top, with climbing roses trained up their sides, is a pleasing and easily constructed ornament. Fancy and taste may range at will in inventing forms to ornament the parterre with roses. Beds of roses, raised pyramidally, have a splendid effect. When the flowers die away in the autumn, the mass may be clipped again into form, with the garden shears, as you would clip a laurel hedge.

Standard roses, which are so much in fashion at this time, and which always remind one of a housemaid's long broom for sweeping cobwebs, are beyond a lady's own management, as budding is a troublesome business, and very frequently fails. I will not, therefore, touch upon that subject.

The *double yellow rose* is very elegant. It requires a western aspect, and even prefers north and east, but a warm aspect injures its beauty. It loves a good substantial soil, and will not bear much cutting or removing. Let it alone in its glory, only pruning away the old scraggy wood occasionally, to strengthen the plant.

The *monthly rose* is also a lover of the north and east. It blooms through the autumn and winter, has an evergreen leaf, and loves a strong soil. It must be propagated by cuttings, and parting the roots, as it never throws up suckers. Prune away the old wood, and make cuttings in June, July, and August, of the branches you clear away. Plant the cuttings in loose, moist earth, and do not let them bud till the following year. Let the cuttings be sunk two joints in the earth, leaving only one exposed. The monthly rose climbs, or creeps.

The *Austrian briar*, or *rose*, will not flower if exposed to the south. It bears a rich mass of flowers, yellow outside, and deep red within. Give it an eastern or western aspect.

The *perpetual*, or "four-season" rose, requires a rich soil. The flower buds appearing in June or July should be pinched off, and in winter the plant may be pruned as closely as its hardier companions. Place the four-season rose in a sheltered situation from winds.

Among the hardy climbing roses, the *Ayrshire rose* is the most useful. Its foliage is rich, and it covers fences, walls, &c., with astonishing rapidity. It flowers in July. Place it in a warm situation, and it will extend thirty feet in one season.

Lady Banks's yellow rose is a pretty climber, and flowers early in all situations. So does the *Rosa sempervirens.*

Climbing roses will grow luxuriantly under the shade of trees, and form a mass of fragrant underwood in shrubberies. They grow with surprising vigor if allowed to remain prostrate. Plant these thinly, and lay in the most vigorous shoots, by pegging them down into the ground. This process increases the plants rapidly, and gives the gayest possible effect.

The *Rosa hybrida multiflora* is a hardy and rapidly growing rose. It flowers also from June to September. So does the red and crimson Boursault, and the *Rosa Russeliana.*

Roses are subject to the green fly, which disfigures their beauty, particularly the white roses. An excellent remedy for this annoyance is effected by moistening the plant, and then dusting it over with equal portions of sulphur and tobacco dust.

The following list of roses will not prove beyond a lady's management, being hardy, and requiring only pruning every January, and giving them a good soil. Prune the white rose-trees very sparingly, as they do not love the knife:—

Roses, early cinnamon
Double yellow
Single yellow
Red monthly
White monthly
Double white
Moss Provence
Common Provence
Double velvet
Single Ditto
Dutch hundred-leaved
Blush ditto
Blush Belgic
Red ditto
Marbled
Large royal
York and Lancaster
Red damask

Blush ditto
Austrian, with flowers having one side red and the other yellow
White damask
Austrian yellow
Double musk
Royal virgin
Rosa mundi, *i. e.*, rose of the world, or striped red rose
Frankfort
Cluster blush
Maiden blush
Virgin, or thornless
Common red
Burnet leaved
Scotch, the dwarf
Striped Scotch
Apple-bearing
Single American
Rose of Meux
Pennsylvanian
Red cluster
Burgundy rose
Perpetual, or four-season

HARDY CLIMBING ROSES.

The Ayrshire rose
Double ditto
Rose hybrida multiflora
Rose Clair
Rosa Russeliana
Reversa elegans
Rosa sempervirens, three sorts
Rose ruga
Red Boursault
Crimson ditto
Lady Banks' yellow rose

JASMINES.

Jasmines grow in very irregular forms. Perhaps their luxuriant wild appearance constitutes their chief grace. The jasmine is a beautiful screen in summer, wreathing its festoons through trellis-work; and it appears to me that Nature presents not, in our colder climes, a more fragrant and beautiful bouquet than a mixture of roses and jasmines.

The common jasmine is hardy, and loves a good soil, by which term I mean kitchen garden soil. Trench round the stem occasionally to lighten the earth, and it will grow very freely. Put litter round the jasmine in severe frost; and if a very rigorous season destroy the branches, the root will be saved, and its shoots in the spring will soon replace the loss. If they shoot out with displeasing irregularity and confusion, take off the least healthy looking branches, and cut away those which grow *rumpled*, for they only consume the juices of the plant to no purpose. The common jasmine is propagated by layers and slips.

The *Arabian jasmine* is very fragrant, but it does not endure cold, or much heat, therefore an eastern aspect suits it best. If the Arabian jasmine is grown in a large pot or box, it could be placed under cover during frost in the winter months; but do not place it in a green-house, which would be in the other extreme again.

The *yellow jasmine* may be treated like the common jasmine. It is not very fragrant, but it forms an elegant variety.

I have seen very fanciful and beautiful devices invented to display the beauty of the jasmine. Their shoots grow so rapidly and luxuriantly, that if the plant is allowed to luxuriate, it will soon cover any frame-work with its drooping beauty. The jasmine loves to hang downwards; and I have admired inventive little arbors, where the plant has been trained up behind them, and the branches allowed to fall over their front in the richest profusion, curtained back like the entrance of a tent. The effect, during their time of flowering, was remarkably elegant.

When you prune the jasmine, cut the branches to an eye or bud, just by the place from which they sprout, and that in such a manner, that the head when trimmed, should resemble the head of a willow. This method makes them throw out abundance of branches and fine flowers.

Give fresh soil to the jasmine every two years, or they will gradually become weakened in their blooms. The secret of having fine flowers is in keeping up the soil to a regular degree of strength, as the human frame languishes under change of diet, and becomes weakened for want of food. Thus it is with animate and inanimate nature.

CHAPTER VII.

ORNAMENTAL SHRUBS AND EVERGREENS.

I SHALL speak now of the ornamental shrubs which decorate a flower garden, and which a lady may *superintend* herself, if her own physical powers are not equal to the fatigue of planting. A laborer, or a stout active girl, may act under her orders, and do all that is necessary to be done, in removing or planting flowering shrubs and evergreens.

In planting flowering shrubs, be very particular to plant them at such distances that each plant may have plenty of room to grow, and strike out their roots and branches freely. If shrubs are crowded together, they become stunted in growth, and lanky in form.

If you are forming a clump, or even a plantation, let each shrub be planted six feet apart from its neighbor: but if you wish to plant roses, syringas, honeysuckles, lilacs, &c., in your flower borders, they should be from twelve to fifteen feet distant from each other, so as not to interfere with the flowers growing below them.

Do not plant tall shrubs promiscuously among low-growing ones. Let the taller shrubs form the back-grounds, that each shrub may be distinctly seen. The shrubs should be trained up with single stems, and they should be pruned every year, taking up the suckers, and removing disorderly branches.

By allowing each shrub plenty of room, it will form a handsome head, and throw out vigorous shoots. You will also have space to dig between the shrubs, and the sun and air can benefit them.

Some of the more beautiful evergreens look extremely well dotted about the grounds singly or in clumps, but be very particular in planting your shrubs.

For instance, when you wish to transplant or plant a shrub, dig a circular hole sufficiently large to receive the roots of the plant, which must be laid neatly down, while some person holds the shrub in its proper position, straight and upright. Cut away any dead or damaged roots; then break the earth well with your spade, and throw it into the hole, shaking the plant gently, just to let the earth fall close in among the roots. When it is well filled up, tread the earth gently round the shrub to fix it, but do not stamp it, as I have seen people do.

But if you can take up shrubs with a ball of earth round their roots, they do not feel the operation, and their leaves do not droop. Water each shrub after planting: give each of them a good soaking, and let each plant have a stake to support it during the winter.

October is the autumn month for transplanting shrubs, and February and March are the spring months. I always prefer the autumn transplanting, as the rains and showers are so fructifying. March is the last month for transplanting evergreens.

Laurustinus, Phillyreas, and Laurel, are excellent shrubs to plant near buildings, or to hide a wall. They are evergreen summer and winter, very hardy, and quick growing.

The Pyracantha is an elegant shrub, with its clusters of red berries; and it looks gay during the autumn and winter.

The Arbutus, or strawberry tree, is loaded with its strawberries in August, September and October. This is a beautiful shrub, placed singly on a lawn, kept to one single clean stem, and a fine branching head.

Portugal laurels are beautiful: their deep green leaves, and scented feathery flowers, make them an important shrub in all gardens.

It has been ascertained by the late severe winter, that evergreens are extremely hardy, and will bear any severity of frost. All those evergreens considered most tender, such as Portugal laurels, rhododendrons, &c., were observed to brave the frost unhurt, which were placed in high unsheltered places, or facing the east and north. It was observed, also, that those evergreens were destroyed whose aspect was south and west, and which lay in warm and sheltered situations. The cause was this. The shrubs did not suffer which were not subject to *alternations* of heat and cold; while those which lay in warm situations, being thawed by the sun's rays during the day, could not endure the sudden chill of returning frost at night.

Plant your evergreens, therefore, fearlessly in exposed situations; and care only, in severe winters, for those which are likely to be thawed and frozen again twice in twenty-four hours.

Rhododendrons are very beautiful shrubs, and grow into trees, if the soil agrees with them. They love a bog soil.

The Camelia japonica is considered a green-house plant, but it becomes hardy, like the laurel, if care is taken to shelter it for a few winters, when it gradually adapts itself to the climate. This is troublesome, perhaps, as most things are, to indolent people; but the trouble is well repaid by the beautiful flowers of the japonicas, its dark leaves, and delicate scent.

The gum Cistus is a handsome evergreen, and looks well anywhere and everywhere. Some straw litter spread round their roots in winter is a great protection.

All evergreens of a hard-wooded nature are propagated rapidly by layers in June or July. This is the method:—Dig round the tree or shrub, and bend down the pliable branches; lay them into the earth, and secure them there with hooked or forked sticks. Lay down all the young shoots on each branch, and cover them with earth about five inches deep, leaving the tops out about two, three, or four inches above ground, according to their different lengths. If these branches are laid in June or July, they will root by Michaelmas; but if they are laid in October, they will be a twelvemonth rooting.

The layers of Alaternuses and Phillyreas will sometimes be two years rooting, if done so late as October; therefore lay down your shoots, if possible, in June. Let the shoots which are layered be those of the last summer's growth.

You may propagate shrubs also from cuttings in February and October. Let strong shoots be chosen, of last summer's growth: choose them from nine to fifteen inches long, and, if you can, take about two inches of old wood with the shoots at their base. Trim off the lower leaves, place the cuttings half way in the ground, and plant them in a shady border to root. Do this in February, in *preference* to October, as everything roots earlier from spring operations. You may also plant cuttings in June, but keep them moist and shady.

October is a good month for taking up suckers of lilacs, roses, &c., and for all sorts of transplanting in its varieties. It is also the month to transplant the layers of such shrubs as were laid in the previous October.

I subjoin a list of hardy deciduous shrubs and evergreens, not too tall to admit into a moderately sized flower garden:—

DECIDUOUS SHRUBS OF LESSER GROWTH.

Arbutus, Strawberry tree
- Common
- Double-flowering
- Red-flowering
- Eastern, or Andrachne

Almond, common
- White-flowering
- Early dwarf, single flower
- Double dwarf

Althæa frutex, striped

Red
White
Blue
Purple
Pheasant's eye
Andromeda, striped
Evergreen
Azalea, with red flowers
White
Berberry, common, red fruit
Stoneless, red fruit
White fruit
Bladder-nut, three-leaved
Five-leaved
Broom, the Spanish
Double-flowering
Yellow Portugal
White Portugal
Lucca
Bramble, double-flowering
American upright
White-fruited
Dwarf
Thornless
Chionanthus, Fringe, or Snowdrop tree
Candleberry Myrtle, broad-leaved
Long-leaved
Fern-leaved
Oak-leaved
Cherry, double-blossomed
Cornelian
Dwarf Canada
Currant, with gold and silver-blotched leaves
With gooseberry leaves
Pennsylvanian
Dogwood, the common
Virginia
Great-flowering
Newfoundland
Empetrum, black-berried heath
Guelder Rose, common
Double, or snowball
Carolina
Gold-blotched leaf
Currant-leaved
Hydrangea, white-flowering
Honeysuckle, early red Italian
Early white Dutch
Late Dutch
Late red
Long-blowing
Large scarlet trumpet
Small trumpet
Oak-leaved
Early white Italian
Early red Italian
Ivy, deciduous, or Virginian creeper
Jasmine, the common white
Common yellow Italian
Gold-striped leaved
Silver-striped leaved
Lilac, blue
White
Purple, or Scotch
Persian, with cut leaves
Persian, white-flowered
Persian, blue-flowered
Lonicera, upright Honeysuckle
Red-berried
Blue-berried
Virginian
Tartarian
Mezereon, white
Early red
Late red
Purple
Mespilus, spring-flowering
Lady Hardwick's shrub
Peach, double-flowering
Privet, common
Silver-striped
Yellow-blotched leaves
Ptelea, or American Shrub Trefoil
Pomegranate, single-flowering
Double
Robinia, or false Acacia
Common
Yellow-flowered
Scarlet-flowered, or rose acacia
Caragana
Rhamnus, or Buckthorn
Common
Sea buckthorn
Yellow-berried
Creeping evergreen
Raspberry, double-flowering
Virginian sweet-flowering
Rose, in every variety
Spiræa frutex, common red
Scarlet
White

Sumach, scarlet
Large downy
White
Virginia
Elm-leaved
Myrtle-leaved
Carolina
Syringa, common
Dwarf double-flowerin
Scorpion Senna
Smilax, broad-leaved
Blotched-leaved
Tulip Tree
Tamarisk, the French
German
Viburnum, or Wayfarer
Common
Stripe-leaved
American broad-leaved
Maple-leaved

EVERGREENS.

Alaternus, common
Blotched-leaved
Jagged-leaved, plain
Ditto, striped
Silver-striped
Gold-striped
Cistus, or Rock Rose
Gum Cistus, with spotted flowers
With plain white flowers
Purple sage-leaved
Male Portugal
Bay-leaved gum
With hairy willow leaves
Black poplar-leaved
Waved-leaved
Purple, or true Gum Cistus of Crete, with other varieties
Cytisus, Neapolitan
Canary
Siberian and Tartarian
Laurustinus, common
Broad, or shining-leaved
Rough-leaved
Oval-leaved
Bay, broad-leaved
Narrow-leaved
Phillyrea, the true
Broad-leaved
Privet-leaved
Prickly-leaved
Olive-leaved
Gold-edged
Silver-edged
Rosemary edged
Juniper, common
Swedish
Sclavonian
Canada
Jasmine, evergreen
Pyracantha
Ivy, common
Striped-leaved
Virginian
Irish, or quick-growing
Honeysuckle, evergreen
Rose, the evergreen
Rhododendron, dwarf Rose Bay
Kalmia, olive-leaved
Broad-leaved
Thyme-leaved
Coronilla, narrow-leaved
Broad-leaved
Magnolia, laurel-leaved
Lesser bay-leaved
Arbor Vitæ, common
China
American
Cypress, common upright
Male spreading
Bignonia, the evergreen
Widow Wail
Locust of Montpelier
Medicago, Moon Trefoil
Stonecrop Shrub
Ragwort, the sea
Holly, the common
Carolina broad-leaved
Yellow-berried
Many varieties
Laurels, common
Portugal
Alexandrian
Oak, Ilex, or evergreen
Kermes, or scarlet-bearing

Gramuntian, holly-leaved
Carolina live
Germander, shrubby, of Crete
Euonymus, evergreen Virginia
Virginia Groundsel Tree
Wormwood, lavender-leaved
Spurge, or wood laurel
Knecholm, or Butcher's Broom
Horse-tail, shrubby

In pruning shrubs, be careful to cut out the long rambling shoots of the last summer's growth, which disfigures their appearance. Cut away, also, branches of shrubs which interlace each other, that every shrub may stand clear and well-defined. Take away their suckers, and let each shrub be kept to a single stem, as I have before observed.

CHAPTER VIII.

ON HOUSE AND WINDOW GARDENING.

(BY MR. CHARLES MACKINTOSH.)

THE culture of flowering and sweet-scented plants, as ornaments in human dwellings, has been practiced from such remote antiquity that no one can name the date of its origin. House plants are also a kind of ornaments which all the labors of the most refined art can never exceed or even reach; and hence in the most refined and luxurious states of society, flowers maintain a high place among the leading ornaments; and the assembly-rooms of beauty and fashion, and the banqueting-halls of the noble and the great, would look tame and barren without those most beautiful and most appropriate decorums.

Farther, it is one of the great merits of these lovely productions of nature, that they are for the humble as well as for the high. The humblest window in the most obscure and crowded court of a city may have its flower-pot; and they who are cut off by occupation or other circumstances from the free range of growing nature, may still command a little vegetable kingdom of their own in a few well-selected and carefully-attended flowers.

A species of ornament, which is in its own nature so pleasing and so innocent, which requires far less labor and expense than many other ornaments of very inferior value, and which adapts itself to every imaginable class of society, is surely worthy of the study, the encouragement, and the care of all who seek happiness to themselves, or wish to promote the happiness of others.

That there is no want of love for such plants is evident from the places in which they appear; but the kind and state of the plants very generally show that there is a great want of knowledge, both in their selection and their management. In order to contribute a little to the supplying of this defect, we propose to offer a very brief compendium of what the French and Germans call "Window Gardening;" and in order to render what we state as clear as possible, we shall divide it into several heads, or points.

PLANTS PROPER FOR WINDOW CULTURE.

As the situation of these plants is different from what they occupy in their natural state, it becomes necessary to select such as are capable of accommodating themselves to circumstances; and as the unfavorable circumstances of house plants are chiefly want of free and pure air, and of light, and in those species which are accustomed to long seasons of repose in the winter, to uniform temperature, these circumstances must be kept in mind in the selection. Rooms, especially in crowded cities, are the most unnatural, and, on that account, the very worst situations in which plants can be placed; and therefore, if healthy plants and an abundance of bloom are sought for, variety must be sacrificed.

Plants which will continue healthy for a long time in the confined air of rooms, are generally those which have a peculiar surface, or texture in the foliage: such are many of the *Aloes, Cactuses, Mesembryanthemums,* among what are called succulent plants; and, in a higher temperature, some of the curious *Epiphytæ,* or the natural order *Orchideæ.* We recollect once seeing a very interesting collection of more than two hundred species, growing in a high state of perfection, in the house of an amateur of succulent plants, living in the Grand Sablon at Brussels. The room containing them was fitted up much in the same way as an ordinary library, with abundance of light shelves round the walls, and a large table in the middle of the room, on which were placed the pots containing the plants. At night, the room was lighted up by an elegant glass lamp, and it was heated by one of those ornamental stoves which are so common on the Continent Altogether, it had a very handsome appearance.

The Chinese are very attentive to the house culture of many of the orchideous epiphytæ, and thereby greatly increase the beauty and the fragrance of their apartments; they have them in ornamental vases and baskets, and even suspended in the air, where they last for many years and flower beautifully. Some of them continue in flower for many months, and diffuse the most delightful fragrance during the night.*

The reason why the succulent and epiphytous plants answer so well for house culture is, that their winter is one of drought and not of cold, and that the latter especially have little, and some of them no mould at the roots in their natural situations. But there has been hitherto a prejudice against, or at all events an ignorance of, and want of attention to, the culture of succulent plants in this country. This is unwise; for many of them are exceedingly beautiful, highly fragrant, and better adapted for house culture than any plants whatever. They are singularly curious and varied in their structures; and, generally speaking, they require less light, air, and moisture, than other plants.

Next to them, in point of eligibility for house culture, may be reckoned such plants as have coriaceous leaves, that is, have their leaves firm, and with a smooth and compact epidermis,—such as oranges, pittosporums, myrtles, and others of similar texture; these are found to have organs much better adapted to confined

* *Renanthera coccinea* is one of the finest of these, and was first flowered in this country by the author of this paper.

air than plants which have the leaves small or of delicate texture. Some tribes, as the heaths, the *Epacrideæ,* and the whole race of pinnate leaved and papilionaceous flowered plants, are wholly unfit for house culture.

TREATMENT OF HOUSE PLANTS.

Water, heat, air, and light, are the four essential stimulants to plants; water, heat, and air, to promote growth; and light to render that growth perfect.

Water, heat, and air, man can command at his pleasure by artificial means; but over light, as an element of the perfect growth of plants, we have less control. To be beneficial to plants, light must come directly from the sun; and therefore the plants should be so placed, as that it may act upon them with as little as possible of that refraction and decomposition which it suffers when it passes obliquely through glass, or any other medium except the air. Plants grown in the open air, and with such free exposure to the light as their habits require, not only develop all their parts in their proper form, but their leaves, flowers, and fruits, have their natural colors, odors, and flavors. Plants excluded from light have not their natural color, odor, nor flavor, they make little or no charcoal in the woody part, the leaves are not green, and if they do flower and fruit, which is rarely the case, the flowers are pale and scentless, and the fruit is insipid. This has been proved by many experiments, of which the blanching of celery and endive by earthing up, and that of a cabbage by the natural process of hearting, are familiar instances. A geranium placed in a dark room becomes first pale, then spotted, and ultimately white; and if brought to the light it again acquires its color

If plants kept in the dark are exposed to the action of hydrogen gas, they retain their green color, though how this gas acts has not been ascertained. Some flowers, too, such as the crocus and tulip, are colored though grown in the dark.

Light seems to be fully as essential to plants as air or heat, and while it acts beneficially on the upper surfaces of the leaves, it appears to be injurious to the under surfaces, at least of some plants; for in whatever way a plant is placed, it contrives to turn the upper surfaces of its leaves to the light. Professor Lindley is, we believe, making some experiments on this subject.

Plants in rooms turn not only their leaves, but their branches to the window at which the light enters, and a plant may, by turning it at intervals, be made to bend successively to all sides; but such bendings weaken the plant, and thus it is an excessive or unnatural action. This turning of the plant to the light is always of course in proportion to the brightness of that light as compared with the other sides of the plant. Flowers, too, open their petals to the light, and close them in the dark, or in some cases, as in that of the crocus, when a cloud passes over the sun. The same flower, and also some others, will open their petals to the light of a lamp or candle, and close them again when that is withdrawn.

It follows as a necessary consequence, that in rooms, plants should be placed as near the window as possible, that the windows should have a south exposure, and that they should be as seldom as possible shaded with blinds or otherwise. If placed at a distance from the windows, plants should be frequently changed, and to place them permanently on tables or man el-shelves is bad management.

Air is as necessary to the health of plants as light; but air can find its way where light cannot, and therefore it requires less care from the cultivator. If the air is too close, opening the door and windows produces a change, the warm air escaping at top, and cold air coming in below; but on opening the windows of a warm room in cold weather, care must be taken not to chill the plants by leaving them in the cold current.

The heat of ordinary dwelling-houses is quite enough for such plants as we would recommend for general culture in rooms, only, in very cold weather, the plants should be removed a little further from the windows. The blinds and shutters are usually a sufficient protection during the night; and we may remark that plants in rooms are more frequently killed by too much heat than by too much cold.

Spring and autumn are the times of the year at which window plants require the greatest attention. It is usual to have the plants outside the windows even during the night in the summer season, and kept in the house both night and day in the winter season. In the intermediate seasons of spring and autumn the plants are frequently placed in their summer situation during the day, and it is desirable that then they should be placed in their winter situation during the night. Our climate is so variable at those seasons, that we not only have summer during the day, and winter during the night, but whole days of summer and winter alternating with each other. Sometimes we have warmer days in April than in May or June, and occasionally we have more severe frosts in the beginning of September, than any which occur again till November is nearly over. Now it is not the absolute heat or cold, but the rapidity of the transition from one to the other which is injurious to plants, and therefore it is absolutely necessary for all such as would have their house plants in the perfection of beauty, to attend to those circumstances. This is more especially necessary in towns, where the people are much less interested in the changes of the weather, and therefore much less observant of them than they are in the country; and we have no doubt that more plants are destroyed from want of attention to those variable periods of the year than from any other cause. It is a safe rule to trust no plant less hardy than a common *Geranium* out-side the window all night, earlier than about the twentieth of June, or later than the first of September. No doubt there are many nights before the first of these times, and after the latter, during which the plants might remain in the open air without injury. There is, however, no knowing what a night may bring forth at those inconstant seasons, and therefore the safe plan is not to leave the plants to chance.

When, as often happens, plants get slightly injured by rost, cold water should be sprinkled on them before the sun reaches them, and this sprinkling ought to be continued as long as any appearance of frost remains on the foliage.

Water is often very injudiciously applied to plants in rooms, and the evil arises from falling into the opposite extremes of too much and too little. Fear of spoiling the carpet, forgetfulness, and sometimes a dread of injuring the plant, are the chief causes of an under supply of water. On the other hand, many have a notion that such plants should be watered every day, or at stated periods, without inquiring whether it be necessary or not. Saucers or pans are often placed under flower-pots to prevent the water, which escapes, from soiling the apartment, but in these cases the saucers should be partly filled with gravel, to prevent the roots from being soaked with water, or the water which lodges in the saucer should be removed.

Fanciful and elegant baskets of wire or wicker-work, and plant-tables are, perhaps, preferable to common stages. The baskets should have a pan, of zinc, copper, or other metal, and over this a bottom pierced with holes, or a grating of wire, on which the pots are to be placed. The pan is generally about an inch deep, and has a plug or other contrivance by which the surplus water may be drawn. Plant-tables can be constructed in the same manner, and admit of an endless variety of forms, according to the taste of the owner. In either of these the pots may be wholly concealed by green moss, or cut paper, so that nothing but the plants themselves may appear.

Water is as essential to the whole plant as it is to the roots, because they are liable to collect dirt, and thereby to be injured; they should, therefore, be frequently washed over with a syringe having a rose to it, and in order to perform this operation properly, the plants must generally be removed to some other apartment where they should remain till they are dry. In winter this operation must be performed in mild weather only; it should be done in an apartment not colder than that in which the plants usually stand, and the water should be about milk warm. When the plants are in baskets or on tables, they can be removed and washed without deranging their order. Plants which have large and leathery leaves, such as oranges, pittosporums, camellias, and myrtles, may be washed with a sponge, or if very foul they may be washed with soap, and the soap carefully removed by pure water. Loose dust may be removed by a pair of bellows. Attention to cleanliness greatly increases the vigor of the plant.

House plants are greatly benefited by being placed out of doors in the summer months, especially during gentle showers; and such as have no other convenience may advantageously place them outside the windows. They may also be syringed and washed in this position, and if the owner is not in possession of one, a common watering-pot, held high, so that the water may fall on the plant with considerable force, is a tolerable substitute.

Plants respire by their leaves, as animals do by their breathing apparatus, and it is on this account that keeping the leaves clean is so very essential to the health of plants. Indeed, the dust which collects on them, and interrupts their respiration, is one of the greatest evils which can befall plants, especially in rooms and on balconies in towns. The respiring pores are generally large in proportion as the leaves are so; and this is one of the reasons why delicate-leaved plants are not so well adapted for house culture as those which have the leaves larger and firmer.

Light has also a considerable effect in promoting the healthy action of leaves, and many plants fold up their leaves in the dark, or even when the sky is lowering. This, though it has no resemblance to sleep in animals, has been called the sleep of plants, and the curious reader may find an interesting notice of it in the "Amœnitates Academicæ" of Linnæus.

THE SUPPLY OF HOUSE PLANTS.

There are many ways of doing this; but to those who have the opportunity, and choose to be at the expense, there is, perhaps, none better than that of contracting for the year with some skilfull and respectable nurseryman; in this case the plants will be attended by the contractor, and kept in the best condition. Much pleasure is, however, sacrificed by those who adopt this mode, inasmuch as the chief enjoyment of plants arises from the feeling that they are the nurslings of our own care; and it is astonishing how strongly the judicious treatment of plants leads to judicious management in all other matters.

Plants, except such as are novelties and sought only by the curious, may always be had at moderate prices from respectable growers. Covent Garden furnishes an abundant supply for London, and those who are not so particular may have them of the hawkers. In dealing with these people, some care is however necessary; very many of the plants which they offer for sale are thrown away or stolen, and in both cases they are taken up without any regard to the preservation of the roots, and thus there is a considerable chance against their success. Those injured plants are made to look healthy for a little time by means of an over supply of water, but they soon languish in the possession of the purchasers.

Another very hazardous mode of purchasing plants is at those sales which are very frequently got up in the spring and autumn. At these, purchasers have no security that the plant is healthy, or that it is what it professes to be, and thus they often pay a higher price for a worthless article in a diseased state, than a regular nurseryman would charge them for a good plant in the finest condition. Such a nurseryman has always character at stake, but the other parties, generally speaking, have none.

MANAGEMENT OF BULBS IN GLASSES.

This is a favorite mode of house culture, and the bulbs best adapted for it are hyacinths, polyanthus-narcissus, Van Thol, and other tulips, crocus, Persian iris, narcissus, colchicum, Guernsey lily, jonquil, and others.

Spring-flowering bulbs are usually purchased in September, and the autumnal ones in July and August, and the largest and best-formed bulbs should be chosen; an abundant supply may be obtained at little cost at the seed-shops and nurseries. To be blown in winter or spring, the bulbs are placed in water in October, and so on in succession till February or March; and for autumn and early winter, they are placed in the water in August and September. Dark-colored glasses are the best, as they prevent the light from decomposing the roots of the plants. Rain water is preferable to any other, and it should be changed frequently, not less than once every third or fourth day, to prevent its getting putrid; and in performing this operation care must be taken both in withdrawing and in replacing the roots. This is necessary only till the flowers have expanded; for after this the plants may be left undisturbed until the flowers have decayed.

The water which is supplied must not be colder than that which is withdrawn, or than the general temperature of the apartment. Much heat is not necessary for such plants, because they flower better the more slowly their vegetation proceeds. Chimney-pieces and other warm situations are not nearly so well adapted for those bulbs as stages near the window, or the window-sill itself.

A better mode of growing those bulbs than the common mode in glasses, would be in a table with a deep pan, and a wire grating on the top. This might be placed about nine inches from the bottom of the pan, and the roots arranged on it, the taller ones in the center, and those of more lowly growth towards the sides. The water in the pan might be drawn off by a plug, and fresh water supplied, without in the least disturbing the plants.

Bulbs may also be grown in fine white sand, kept constantly moistened, and in this way very beautiful blooms may be obtained.

NOSEGAYS AND CUT FLOWERS.

Though these are very acceptable to most persons, there are few who rightly understand the art of keeping them long in a fresh state, or of reviving them when they have faded. It is true, that when a flower or branch is cut off from its parent plant, its support is thereby destroyed; but still some flowers may be kept in great beauty for a much longer period than others, and many for a far longer time than is generally done, or even supposed possible.

For this purpose, flowers should be gathered early in the morning, but not till the dew be nearly dried off them. They should be placed in a flat basket, or on a tray, so as not to press upon and crush each other; and they should be neatly cut, and not mangled or bruised. When thus gathered, they should be covered with a sheet of paper, and immediately conveyed to the apartment where they are to be used, if that apartment be near at hand. But if they are to be sent to any distance, they should be placed in tin cases, such as botanists use when collecting specimens. We have sent flowers, in such cases, for several hundred miles, and found most of them in good condition at the end of a journey of three or four days' continuance. In this way the Dutch florists send specimens of their finest flowers not only to England, but to more distant parts of continental Europe. Our own florists send to the metropolis, for competition at exhibitions, flowers from Cornwall, from the north of England and from Scotland, and they arrive without the least decay. They are placed in wooden or tin boxes, having an internal arrangement of small phials, fixed under a covering of tin or wood, perforated with holes, just large enough to admit the stalks of the flowers, the ends of which are placed in the water of the phials, and in this way they are conveyed with perfect safety.

Flowers should not be cut during sunshine, or kept exposed to the solar influence; neither should they be collected in large bundles and tied tightly together, as this invariably hastens their decay. When in the room where they are to remain, the ends of the stalks should be cut clean across with a very sharp knife (never with scissors), by which means the tubes through which they draw the water are left open, so that the water ascends freely, which it will not do if the tubes of the stems are bruised or lacerated. An endless variety of ornamental vessels are used for the reception of such flowers, and they are all equally well adapted for the purpose, so that the stalks are inserted in pure water. This water ought to be changed every day, or once in two days at the furthest, and a thin slice should be cleanly cut off from the end of each stalk every time the water is removed, which will occasion fresh action and re·ive the flowers. Water, about milk warm, or containing a small quantity of camphor, will sometimes revive decayed flowers. The best method of applying this, is to have the camphor dissolved in spirits of wine, for which the common camphorated spirits of the druggists' shops will be quite sufficient; and to add a drop or two of this for every half ounce of water. A glass-shade is also useful in preserving flowers; and cut flowers ought always to be shaded during the night, and indeed at all times when they are not purposely exhibited. The following are some of the genera of plants the flowers of which remain longest after being cut:—*Gnaphalium*, *Astelma*, *Helichrysum*, *Phænocoma*, *Aphelexis*, and others, which the French have designated "immortal flowers," from remaining unchanged by decay, hold the first rank. Next to these come the whole natural order, *Proteaceæ*, many of *Gramineæ*, several of *Cruciferæ*, several in *Rhamneaceæ*, several in *Cassuviæ*—the genus *Acacia* in *Leguminosæ*, all *Calycanthaceæ*, most of *Myrtaceæ*, most of *Dipsaceæ*, several of *Compositæ*, most of *Ericeæ*—the genera *Lavendula*, *Sideritis* and *Phlomis*, in *Labiatæ*, all *Orobancheæ*, all *Plumbagineæ*, all *Amaranthaceæ*, many of *Orchideæ*, *Strelitzia*, and *Heliconia* in *Musaceæ*.

INSECTS AND DISEASES OF HOUSE PLANTS.

Plants in rooms, especially geraniums and roses, are very liable to be attacked by aphides. These may be easily removed by tobacco smoke or tobacco water; and where the smell is not offensive, smoke blown from a common tobacco pipe is as effectual as any other method. Camphorated water may be used by those who dislike the smell of tobacco. Mildew, occasionally, though rarely, attacks house plants. It appears like a white powder, and is supposed to consist of minute fungi; but these fungi are not the original disease, but its consequences, and their appearance shows that the plant has been in impure air or otherwise improperly treated. Sulphur or camphor will effectually remove this mildew; and a scaly insect of the coccus tribe, which appears occasionally on oranges, camellias, and similar plants, may be removed by a sponge and water.

Many persons have a dislike to plants in houses as being unhealthy; and as this dislike is in a great measure groundless, we may notice it. Dr. Priestley was the first to show that the leaves of plants absorb carbonic acid gas by their upper surfaces, and give out oxygen by their under ones, thereby tending to purify the air in as far as animal life is concerned; because carbonic acid gas is pernicious to animals, and oxygen is what that life acquires. It is in the light, however, that these operations are carried on; for in the dark, plants give out carbon; and this may be one reason why plants grown in the dark have little or no charcoal in their substance. It does not appear, however, that any of the scentless products given out by plants are injurious to human beings; because those who live among accumulated plants are not less healthy than others; though many persons feel dislike and even pain from the odors of particular plants, in a way not very easily accounted for.

On the Continent in general, and in France and Germany in particular, flowers of all sorts, but particularly the most fragrant, are admitted into the saloons, chambers, and even bed rooms of people of all classes; and they, rather than complain of any ill effects arising from their presence, complain more of the difficulty of procuring them in sufficient abundance. The flowers most in demand for the chambers of the French and Germans are, oranges, jasmine, carnations, honey-suckle, mignonette, olive, rocket, rose, violet, wall-flower, rosemary, stock, lavender, savory, oleander, hyacinth, lilac, syringa, heliotrope, narcissus, &c., all sweet-smelling flowers; and these they indulge in to a very considerable extent.

We may safely conclude, then, that plants admitted into rooms to the extent that they are in general, can produce no effect injurious to the health of persons in general, but, on the contrary, will afford amusement to the mind and exercise to the body, both of which are so necessary towards the enjoyment of good health. The mind will be agreeably exercised in contemplating the beauty of the flowers, but more so still if the study of their respective parts, natures and structures, in a botanical or physiological point of view, be at the same time attended to. An agreeable and rational exercise will be provided for the body, if the proprietor, particularly if of the softer sex, take the entire management of her little *Window Garden* into her own hands.

CHAPTER IX.

DOMESTIC GREENHOUSES.*

BEFORE entering on a description of this apparatus, the circumstances under which it was discovered may be briefly adverted to. Mr. Ward, the gentleman to whom we are indebted for the discovery, is a surgeon, residing in Well-close Square, London. From his earliest youth Mr. Ward has been attached to botanical pursuits; but living in a densely populated neighborhood, surrounded with manufactories, and enveloped in the smoke of London in its very worst form, he had been compelled to give up the cultivation of plants, until the following simple incident seemed to point out a mode by which he could follow his favorite amusement with some degree of success. He had buried the chrysalis of a sphinx in some moist mould, which was inclosed in a glass bottle covered with a top. In watching the bottle from day to day, he observed that when exposed to the warmth of the sun the moisture rose from the mould, and became condensed on the inner surface of the glass, and again fell back upon the mould during the night, thus keeping up a continual moisture in the atmosphere within the glass; he also observed about a week prior to the final change of the insect, a seedling fern and grass appear on the surface of the mould. After having secured the insect, Mr. Ward set himself to observe

* The materials for this paper are chiefly from Chambers's Edinburgh Journal, with some slight additions from Mr. Ellis's paper read to the Botanical Society of Edinburgh.

the development of these plants in this confined situation. He placed the bottle outside the window of his study, where the plants continued for several years to exhibit a healthy vegetation, suggesting at the same time further experiments, which have led to a most extraordinary result, when we consider, that by this simple application of the laws of nature as regards atmosphere, the most forbidding local circumstances may be overcome, and that any person, whether inhabiting the most humble or the most splendid dwelling, provided it be freely exposed for a few hours every day to the sun's light, has it in his power to rear and cultivate a miscellaneous collection of plants, to enjoy the beauty of their appearance, and to watch their progress through all the stages of their growth, at an expense so insignificant as to be within the means of every man even in very moderate circumstances.

To do this he must provide an apparatus consisting of a box, a stand, and a glass roof, of a size according to his desires and means. We shall suppose one is wanted of a small size to stand in a window in an apartment of limited dimensions. The stand,

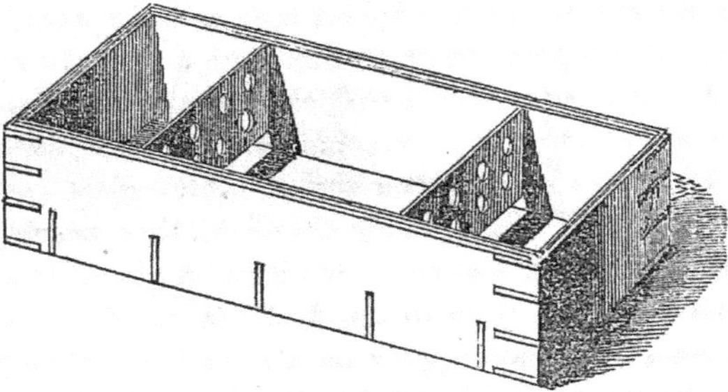

we will suppose, is one foot ten inches in height, the box whic is to contain the mould eight inches and a half, and the glass frame one foot seven inches and a half;—in all four feet two inches in height by three feet in length and a foot and a half in breath. If elegance is aimed at, the box should be made of mahogany, and supported on four legs, furnished with movable castors; the box which is to contain the soil, eight and a half inches in height, should be made of well-seasoned St. Domingo mahogany, steeped in Kyan's composition, for a fortnight; the sides, one and a quarter inches thick, mitered and dove-tailed together at the corners. The bottom of the box should be Honduras mahogany, one inch thick, formed of numerous small pieces,

framed and flush-paneled, and arranged so as best to resist the yielding of the wood. To give it greater strength, two cross pieces or ties stretch from side to side at equal distance from each other; these are dove-tailed on each side, thus dividing the box into three compartments, but leaving open spaces under the ties and holes through their centers to permit the moisture to percolate freely through the whole of the mould. The bottom being properly fitted, the sides are fixed to it with brass nails—no iron being used in any part. When completed and filled with plants, the apparatus appears something like the cut on p. 93.

At the upper edge of the box a groove is sunk to receive the lower edge of the glass roof which rests securely in it. This groove is lined with brass; its inner lip is one sixteenth of an inch lower than the outer, and at each end is a notch one fifth of an inch only above the bottom of the groove to allow the condensed moisture which trickles down the inside of the glass to flow back into the mould.

The frame-work cover of which we have now to speak is made of brass, with a door on one side, made to fit close. The glass used for it may be of flattened crown-glass; that for the door should be plate-glass. The panes must be fitted in the frames with great care, and with a putty specially made for the purpose, which should, when dry, receive three coats of paint. Along the top of the roof, hooks or brass rods may be placed, from which small pots may be suspended. The whole of the frame-work should be well fitted, and nicely put together, so as to preclude as far as possible all interchange between the air in the case and that in the room.

We now come to the preparation for the plants. Lay the bottom of the box with pieces of broken earthenware, to a depth of two inches, as an open subsoil. Next, lay a stratum of turfy loam one inch deep, and fill in the remainder of the space with soil, composed of equal portions of peat and loam, mixed with about one-twentieth part of rough white sand, free from iron The artificial garden-plot is now ready to receive the plants. Plant these in the usual manner, and then shower over them, with a fine rose watering-pot, from three to four gallons of water, till the soil be pretty well saturated, and the liquid begins to run off by the two openings in the bottom. After draining thus for twenty-four hours, cork up the holes, place the glass-case on the box, and the operation will be finished.

After the first preparation, the plants require little or no care; the case need only be opened for the removal of dead leaves, or for a little trimming, when required. Plants in open flower-pots are exposed to the vicissitudes of change of climate, and require constant watering; but the plants in these cases seem to be independent of any change of temperature in the air, and water themselves. The moisture rises by the sun's influence from the moistened earth, cherishes the leaves of the plants in its aerial condition, and during the cool of night falls to the earth again like rain or dew. In this manner there is a constant succession of rising and falling of moisture, in imitation of the great processes of nature, daily going on in the fields around us. The plant-case is a little world in itself, in which vegetation is supported solely by the resources originally communicated to it.

Not the least remarkable part in the economy of the case is the preservation of atmospheric purity. To all who reflect for the first time on this subject, it will seem incomprehensible how the plants can possibly thrive and blossom without the occasional interchange of fresh air with the atmosphere. This certainly does appear extraordinary, yet it is ascertained by experiment that no such reinvigoration is requisite. To account for the phenomena, it will be necessary to explain the constitution of atmospheric air, and the means adopted by nature for its purification.

Air consists of three gases in close mechanical union—nitrogen, oxygen and carbonic acid, in the proportion of about 79 of nitrogen, 20 oxygen, and 1 of carbonic acid, in 100 parts of pure air. In this mixed composition, the essential element for the support of respiration in both animals and plants, and also for combustion, is the oxygen, the nitrogen being little else than a diluent tc modify the strength of the oxygen. It was long believed by men of science that plants possessed the power of exuding oxygen, and so formed a prime agent for restoring vitiated air to purity. Later investigations, however, chiefly by French chemists, have made it evident that plants have no such power, unless when placed under the influence of the sun's rays, or, in other words, that solar light is the grand cleanser of the atmosphere, and without which both plants and animals languish and die. With respect to plants in particular, it is ascertained that, while inhaling oxygen and expiring carbonic acid, their leaves possess the remarkable property, in conjunction with the sun's light, of re-transforming the carbonic acid into oxygen. At night, when the light of day has departed, the expired carbonic acid may be detected in the neighborhood of plants; and hence one cause of injury to health by breathing night air; but when the morning sun again bursts upon the scene, a great chemical process commences in the atmosphere—the carbonic acid is decomposed, oxygen is evolved, and all nature rejoices in a recreation of its appropriate nourishment.

A question will here readily occur—what species of plants are best adapted for these domestic greenhouses? We are fortunately enabled to answer this inquiry by referring to a learned paper on the subject by Mr. Ellis, which was read to the Botanical Society of Edinburgh, January 13, 1839, and afterwards published in the Gardener's Magazine, and also as a separate pamphlet. According to this gentleman's statement, the plants most suitable are "those which partake largely of a cellular structure, and possess a succulent character, and especially those which have fleshy leaves; whilst, on the contrary, the continued humidity is unfavorable to the development of flowers of most exogenous plants, except such as naturally grow in moist and shady situations." Plants, therefore, which have to grow and bloom in cavernous and moist situations, or in moist and warm climates, are best adapted for these cases. However, within this class of vegetables there are many beautiful and highly luxuriant plants, which it would afford no small pleasure to contemplate. The following is a list of plants from various countries, which were set in a box, under Mr. Ellis's directions, and examined from nine to twelve months afterwards :

BOTANICAL NAMES.	COUNTRY.	REMARKS.
Chamæ'rops humilis	Italy, Sicily, Spain	Increased 1-4th its original size
Centi*ana* verna	England	Flowered, but no difference in size
Adiantum Capillus Veneris	England	Increased 1-8th
Primula farinosa	Scotland	Flowered; atmosphere rather damp for it
Primula scotica	Scotland	Flowered; atmosphere rather damp for it
Verbascum Myconi	Scotland	Increased 1-8th
Androsace villosa	Scotland	Flowered; not very healthy
Chamæ'rops *Palmetto*	Carolina	Increased 1-3d
Dionæ'*a* Muscipula	Carolina	Made 1-8th
Sarracen*ia* purpurea	Carolina	Increased 4 times its original size
Epigæ'a repens	Carolina	Increased one-half
Testudinaria elephantipes	Cape of Good Hope	Made a shoot 10 inches long
A'loe retusa	Cape of Good Hope	Made 1-3rd, showing flower spikes
Rhododendron chrysanthum	Siberia	Increased one-half
Chamæcistus	Austria	Increased 1-3d
Cycas revoluta	China	Increased 1-8th
Nepenthes distillatoria	Ceylon	Increased 2-3ds
Cypripedium venustum in-	Nepal	Increased 1-5th
signe	Nepal	Increased 1-4th
Agave geminiflora	Mexico	Increased 1-3d
*Goodyer*a* discolor	Mexico	No perceptible difference
*Echinocactus multiplex	Mexico	Increased one-half
*peruviana	Mexico	Increased one-half
myriacantha	Mexico	Increased one-half
*formosa	Mexico	Increased 1-3d
O'ttoni	Mexico	Increased 1-4th
candida	Mexico	Increased one-half
Epiphyllum truncatum	Brazil	Increased 2-3ds
Cereus flagelliformis	Peru	Increased one-half
Lycopodium stoloniferum	Cuba	Very luxuriant

Those marked thus * are growing in fancy pots, and suspended from the roof of the plant-case.

The alternate action of vitiation and purification is emphatically described as follows by Mr. Ellis, in the pamphlet before us:—"Under a bright sunshine, the two processes by which carbonic acid is alternately formed and decomposed go on simultaneously; and their necessary operation, in as far as regards the condition of the air, is that of counteracting each other. Hence, though both may be continually exercised in favorable circumstances, the effects of neither on the atmosphere can be ascertained by ordinary means; and, consequently, though, in the experiments of De Saussure with common air, the production and decomposition of carbonic acid by plants in sunshine must have been continually going on, yet, in all the analysis which he made, the air was found unchanged, either in purity or volume; in other words, the processes of formation and decomposition of this acid gas exactly counterbalanced each other.

"Of the two processes which have now been described (continues our authority), each may be considered as in its nature and purpose quite distinct from the other; hence their efforts may be readily distinguished; neither do they necessarily interfere, when actually working together. The first or deteriorating process, in which oxygen gas is consumed, goes on at all times and in all circumstances when vegetation is active. It requires always a suitable temperature in which to display itself; and when that temperature falls below a certain point, which is very variable in regard to different plants, the process is more or less completely suspended, again to be renewed when the temperature shall return. This conversion of oxygen into carbonic acid is as necessary to the evolution of the seed as to the growth of the plant, and is all that is required for germination. But the plant requires something more; for if light be excluded, vegetation proceeds imperfectly, and the plant does not then acquire its proper color and other active properties which it ought to have. The chief organs by which the consumption of oxygen gas is effected are the leaves; and its purpose, in great part at least, seems to be that of producing some necessary change in the sap during its transmission through those organs, on its way from the vessels of the wood to those of the inner bark, whereby it may be rendered fit for the purposes of nutrition and growth. In its nature and object, therefore, as well as in the specific change which it produces in the air, this process closely resembles the function of respiration in animals, and may thus with propriety be deemed a physiological process. The second, or purifying process, in which oxygen gas is evolved, differs in all respects from that which has just been described. It is in a great measure independent of temperature; at least it proceeds in temperatures too low to support vegetation, provided light be present—an agent not required for germination, nor essential to vegetable development. The organs by which this process acts on the air are, as before, the leaves; not, however, by changing the qualities of the sap in the vessels of those organs, but by producing changes in the chromule, or colorable matter, in their cells, to which it imparts color and other active properties. In doing this, it does not convert the oxygen gas of the air into carbonic acid, but, by decomposing that acid gas, restores to the air the identical portion of oxygen of which the former process had deprived it. The former process, carried on by the agency of the oxygen gas of the air, was essential to living action, and affected the well-being of the whole plant; that exercised by the agency of light is not necessary to life, is local, not general in its operation, and is capable of proceeding in circumstances and under conditions incompatible with living action. By withdrawing the air altogether, or depriving it of oxygen gas, vegetation soon ceases through the whole plant; but the exclusion of light from any part of the plant affects that part only; and even the total exclusion of that agent only deprives the plant of certain properties necessary to its perfection, but not essential to its life. These differences in the processes by which oxygen gas is alternately consumed and evolved, during the vegetation of plants in sunshine, are so manifest, both in their nature and effects, as to satisfy the ascription of a name to the latter process distinct from that given to the former. It might, perhaps, be denominated the chemical process, in contradistinction to that named physiological.

"It would contribute much, we think, to simplify our inquiries concerning vegetation, to bear in mind these distinctions; to consider the one process as accomplished by the agency of the air, and essential to the life and growth of the plant; the other, as subordinate, depending on the agency of light, and though necessary to the perfection of vegetation, yet not essential to its existence. In this manner each process may be followed out separately, both in regard to its immediate effects and remoter consequences, without clashing with the other; and the apparently discordant and even contradictory phenomena which on a first view they seem to exhibit, may be reconciled, and considered, not less in theory than in fact, as conspiring together to form one harmonious and perfect whole."

After these explanations, little need be added respecting the supply of pure air to domestic greenhouses. The deterioration of the atmosphere in the case is daily counteracted by an opposite process of purification, so that amidst the vicissitudes of perpetual change, the air is maintained in a state of nearly uniform composition and purity, and serves over and over again for all the purposes of vegetation. It may, however, be stated, to prevent misconception, that the more pure the air of the apartment, the plants will have the better chance of thriving, because there must necessarily be an interchange to some extent betwixt the air of the room and the case, in consequence of the daily expansion from heat, and nightly condensation from cold. This interchange will be effected by the minute crevices in the apparatus, and therefore requires no special provision.

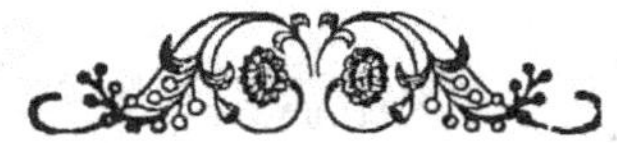

CHAPTER X.

MONTHLY NOTICES.

A RECAPITULATION of the work which each month presents to the gardener's notice will be useful. By occasionally glancing over the Monthly Notices, the memory is refreshed; and it will be found that even the three winter months allow the young gardener no remission from labor. There is something to be done in every week in the year—something to be attended to, which amuses the mind, interests the imagination, and benefits the general tone of mental and physical health.

JANUARY.

Let your *lawn* and *grass walks* be kept neat and smooth, by rolling, this month; and if any part of the grounds require fresh turf, this is the season for cutting and laying it down. If you live in the neighborhood of a common, that is the best ground for cutting turf, as the herbage is short, and free from nettles, docks, &c. Lay it down firm and even, allowing for the sinking of the newly-laid earth, about an inch or two. Roll it well, after having laid down the turf.

Keep the *gravel walks* also from weeds and moss, and roll them in dry weather. If you attempt to roll gravel in wet weather, the gravel clings to the roller.

Dig the clumps or spots where you mean to plant evergreens, in February and March, that the ground may be trenched in readiness. The frost of this month will render newly-dug earth more friable, and the snow will enrich it.

If the weather is very settled and mild, you may still plant out hardy deciduous shrubs, such as sweetbriars, double bramble, double-blossomed cherry, dwarf almond, jasmines, honeysuckles, roses, lilacs, laburnums, guelder rose, Spiræa frutex, mezereons, &c. Transplant each shrub with a good ball of earth round its roots.

Prune flowering shrubs now, where they require it, with a sharp knife, not with shears. When I say "flowering shrubs," I do not mean shrubs *in* flower, but shrubs that *do* flower.

Transplant suckers from the hardy flowering shrubs, if they have not been done before. Take them up with good roots, and support them neatly with stakes.

Cuttings of young shoots of hardy deciduous shrubs may be planted in mild weather, to root, and form good plants in the autumn. Layers may be also formed.

Protect all the choicer kinds of flowering shrubs, and all cuttings of every kind, from severe frosts, by spreading litter over them.

Plant tulips now—always providing the weather is mild—to blow late in the year; but they will not be so handsome as those which were planted again in September and October.

Plant any ranunculuses, anemones, &c., you may have out of the ground, to come in late blowing; but, like the tulips, they will not bear such fine blooms. Protect everything from severe weather, as well as you can, this month, particularly your choicer sorts of bulbs, and tuberous-rooted perennials.

FEBRUARY.

February is the first spring month, and the parterre will begin to make gradual approaches to gaiety and life. The anemones, hepaticas, &c., will now bud and flower, if the weather is genial; and the crocus and snowdrop will put forth their blooms to meet the sun on his returning march.

About the end of this month, you may begin to sow the hardy annuals. I prefer April, but it may not be ccnvenient always to wait so long; therefore sow now the seeds of hawkweed, lavatera, Venus's looking-glass, Venus's navelwort, candytuft, larkspurs, lupines, convolvulus, flos Adonis, dwarf lychnis, nigelia, annual sunflowers, &c.

This month, you may plant and transplant, fearlessly, all hardy, fibrous-rooted flowering perennials and biennials, such as saxifrage, gentianella, hepaticas, violets, primroses of all sorts, polyanthuses, double daisies, thrift, &c.; rose campions, rockets, campanulas, sweet-williams, hollyhocks, scarlet lychnis, carnations, pinks, monk's-hood, perennial asters and sunflowers, &c.

Plant cuttings of roses, honeysuckles, and jasmines.

If the weather is mild, you may transplant many kinds of evergreen shrubs, such as phillyreas, alaternuses, laurels, laurustinus, pyracanthas, cistuses, &c. Let there be a ball of earth round their roots, when you take them out of the ground.

If box edging is required, plant it now; water it, and the plants will soon root.

Dig the borders, carefully and lightly, with your garden fork; make the garden look neat, and free from weeds; clear away dead leaves; sweep the lawn and walks; and let spring advance in its proper order.

MARCH.

Now plant away. Evergreens cannot be moved at a better period. Deciduous flowering shrubs may also be still planted, such as Althæa frutex, syringas, roses, honeysuckles, mezereons, sumach, laburnums, lilacs, jasmines, candleberry myrtles, guelder roses, &c.

Where the borders require filling up, the following plants may still be moved, but do it early in this month :—

Lychnises, campanulas, Canterbury bells, tree primroses, rockets, sweet-williams, wallflowers, columbines, monk's-hood, rose campions, perennial asters and sunflowers, foxgloves, &c.

Sow perennial and biennial flower seeds about the last week in this month. Stake your hyacinths, when the flower stems are tall.

Plant out layered carnations of last year, into the places where they ought to remain.

Give fresh earth to any plants in pots, such as carnations, pinks, auriculas, double sweet-williams, double stock gillyflowers, rockets, &c.

Sow annuals of all hardy kinds.

Transplant any hardy roses, which you may wish should blow late in the year.

Plant box, for edgings, still; and roll the lawn and grass walks.

Transplant any tenderer kinds of annuals which you may have been at the pains of raising in, or procuring *from*, a hot-bed.

Keep the garden quite free from weeds and dead leaves.

APRIL.

Now place sticks to every plant or stalk requiring support. Fix the sticks, or light iron rods, firmly in the ground; and tie the stems to each stick neatly, in two or three places.

Some *evergreens* may yet be removed, as laurels, laurustinus, Portugal laurel, cistuses, arbutus, magnolias, pyracanthas, &c.

Propagate auriculas, by slipping off their suckers and offsets, this month.

Sow carnation and polyanthus seeds still. Sow, also, perennial and biennial seeds.

Where any perennial or biennial fibrous-rooted flowers are wanted, transplant them only in the first week of this month, and they must have each a good ball of earth attached to them; but this work should be completed in February, or March at farthest.

Every sort of annual may now be sown.

Take care of your hyacinths, tulips, ranunculuses, and anemones now, for they will be hastening into bloom.

Place your auriculas, hyacinths, &c., which may be in pots, in a sheltered place, during heavy rains or winds; and shelter those flowers which are in the borders as well as you can. Trim them from dead leaves.

Keep your lawn and grass walks nicely mown and rolled, and your borders free from weeds and rubbish.

MAY.

Propagate perennial fibrous-rooted plants by cuttings.

Propagate double wall-flowers by slips of the young shoots of the head.

Sow annuals for succession; such as sweet-peas, nasturtiums, lavatera, lupines, flos Adonis, &c.

Take up those hyacinths, tulips, &c. which have done flowering, and dry them in the shade to put away.

Weeds grow quickly now: hoe them up wherever you see them. Support all flowers with sticks; train them upright. Clear away all the dead leaves from your carnations, and gently stir the earth round them with your smallest trowel.

Look round the borders now, and take off irregular shoots.

JUNE.

Propagate carnations by layers and pipings. Propagate double sweet-williams and pinks by layers and cuttings, or slips.

Propagate perennial fibrous-rooted plants by cuttings of the stalks.

Transplant the large annuals from the seedling bed to the places where they are to remain. Let this be done in showery weather, if possible.

Take up all bulbs, ranunculuses, and anemone roots, &c., as the flowers and leaves decay.

Water the delicate plants, if the weather proves dry: give a moderate watering every evening, but never in the heat of the day.

Sow yet some hardy annuals, such as ten-week stocks, virgin stock, &c.

Plant out China-asters, Chinese hollyhocks, ten-week stocks, large convolvolus, &c., but let each root have a ball of earth round it.

Examine the perennial and biennial plants, to cut off all dead, broken, or decaying shoots. Trim the African and French marigolds from their lower straggling shoots, that they may present a neat, upright appearance. Trim the chrysanthemums, which are apt to branch too near the root, and stake them neatly.

Plant out carnations and pink seedlings into their proper places.

Keep everything just moderately moist, if there is a long drought in this month.

JULY.

You may lay carnations and double sweet-williams still; but let it be done before the end of the second week in this month.

Propagate pinks by slips and pipings

Transplant the seedling auriculas which were sown last year, as also the seedling polyanthus.

Transplant the perennial and biennial seedlings which were not done last month, to remain till October.

Take up all bulbs as fast as they decay their leaves. If this month prove hot and dry, place your potted carnations in a sheltered situation, and keep them just moist.

Support flowering shrubs and plants, and cut away decayed stems. Keep the borders clean. Mow the lawn and grass walks. Plant autumnal bulbs.

AUGUST.

You may now begin to propagate some double-flowered and approved fibrous-rooted plants the end of the month, if they have done flowering—such, for instance, as the double rose campion, catchfly, double scarlet lychnis, double rocket, double ragged robin, bachelor's buttons, gentianella, polyanthuses, auriculas, &c.

Sow auricula and polyanthus seed on a warm, dry day; and remove carnation layers to some place where they may remain till October to gain strength.

Sow seeds of bulbs.

Sow anemone and ranunculus seed.

Remove all bulbs which have done flowering.

Cut and trim edgings of box. Clip holly, yew, and privet hedges.

Gather flower seeds.

Plant autumnal bulbs, if any are still above ground, such as colchicums, autumnal narcissus, amaryllis, and autumn crocus.

Trim the flower plants; mow the lawn and grass walks, and keep every department in neat order.

SEPTEMBER.

Transplant, in any moist or showery weather this month, the perennial and biennial seedlings to their proper situations, with a ball of earth round their roots.

Propagate fibrous-rooted plants.

Prepare the spots where you mean to deposit anemone and ranunculus roots any time between the end of this month and the end of October; and dig all beds and borders which are vacant, to prepare them also for receiving roots and plants next month.

Transplant peonies, flag irises, monk's-hood, fraxinella, and such like plants, to part their roots and remove each root to its destined position.

Transplant evergreens.

Plant cuttings of honey-suckles, and other shrubs.

Plant hyacinth and tulip roots for early spring bloom.

Plant box by slips or roots.

Mow grass lawn and walks. Clear away flower stems, and trim flowering plants.

Sow seeds of bulbous flowers, if not done last month.

OCTOBER.

This is a very busy month; for the garden should now be cleared and arranged for the season.

Transplant all sorts of fibrous-rooted perennial and biennial plants now where they are intended to remain.

Put the bulbs into the ground again; and transplant the different layered plants into their respective places.

Prune flowering shrubs of all sorts. Plant and transplant all hardy deciduous shrubs, and their suckers.

Dig up and part the roots of all flowers which require so doing, and replant them.

Plant cuttings of honeysuckles, laurels, &c.

Take up the roots of dahlias, and put them carefully away till May.

Trim evergreens.

Plant box edgings; cut away the long, sticky roots, and trim the tops even.

Mow grass walks and lawns, and weed gravel walks.

NOVEMBER.

Prepare compost for a new year by raking dead leaves, soil, sand, &c., in a heap, to turn well over occasionally. Pour the brine, soap-suds, &c., from the house over it.

Transplant still all hardy kinds of flowering shrubs, suckers, &c.

Clear the borders from dead annuals, leaves, stumps, &c.; shelter the choice bulbs and double-flowering plants.

DECEMBER.

Take care of every thing. Protect the more delicate roots from severe frost, by strewing ashes, sand, or litter over them. Prune shrubs, and dig between them.

If the weather is open, you may still plant hardy sorts of flowering shrubs.

INDEX.

CPSIA information can be obtained
at www.ICGtesting.com
Printed in the USA
BVHW030238060820
585672BV00001B/32

9 781429 013840